Advance Praise for
Youth Ministry in the Black Church:
Centered in Hope

"Committed youth advocates Wimberly, Barnes, and Johnson offer a passionate, timely, valuable, and interactive resource centered in hope. This book is a much welcomed and important addition to ministry studies focused on the black church. Youth leaders, Christian educators, pastors, undergraduate and graduate students in youth ministry, as well those passionate about ministry with black youth should read this book."—**Rev. Richelle B. White, PhD, Associate Professor of Youth Ministry, Director of Youth Ministry Field Practicum, Kuyper College**

"When it comes to youth ministry, there are basic principles that transcend culture, ethnicity, and even international borders. Also needed, however, is the 'backstory'—the complex mix facing youth ministry leaders in the black church today. Coming from extensive conversations with youth ministry leaders in black churches, the authors weave a narrative that answers the real-life questions asked by AA seminarians." —**Dr. R. Allen Jackson, New Orleans Baptist Theological Seminary**

"Empowering hope-filled youth ministries is the gift of this amazing and concrete book, *Youth Ministry in the Black Church*. Through ethnographic research, the authors share the realities that make a difference in the lives of youth and congregations. Assessment and planning activities assist the reader to critically reflect on her or his ministry and explore God's hope in practice. The book's focus on 'village power' is an added blessing. We all have a responsibility to teach, nurture, invite, and empower youth to live, as the authors' say, the 'God thing' emerging in our lives. Read this book and engage transcending hope." —**Jack L Seymour, Professor of Religious Education, Garrett-Evangelical Theological Seminary; Editor, RELIGIOUS EDUCATION**

"Where was this book when I was getting started? It's an incredible tool for helping the black church understand youth ministry. This volume isn't just for youth pastors; it's a must-read for anybody in church leadership. Today's black church needs this book in going forward in the future." —Maina Mwaura, Youth Pastor, Greenforest Community Baptist Church

"Never to disappoint, Wimberly and her colleagues offer a multi-textured understanding of youth ministry in the black church as hope-centered in its adult leadership, congregational support, and practices with teenagers. This resource is clear, concrete, and challenging to youth ministry leaders who are called to 'foster a future of hope' with black youth." —Evelyn L. Parker, PhD, Associate Professor of Practical Theology, Perkins School of Theology, Southern Methodist University

"The importance of youth ministry within the black church in the United States has acquired even greater importance as the means by which youth can be nurtured within the formational, emancipatory power of black Christian faith. *Youth Ministry in the Black Church* brings together the combined talents of the authors, whose expertise spans the interdisciplinary areas of Christian education, the social sciences, and practical youth ministries. This text provides a comprehensive overview of youth ministry, offering a rich panoply of resources and research findings that will be of great assistance to all who are interested in supporting and empowering black youth in these complex and challenging times." —Anthony G. Reddie, PhD, Editor of *Black Theology: An International Journal,* and Author, *SCM Core Text: Black Theology*

"*Youth Ministry in the Black Church: Centered in Hope* is a must-read for pastors, Christian educators, and youth leaders. The authors have woven their expertise in Christian education and youth ministry with experiences of youth and youth leaders from various church traditions. This book challenges the reader to develop ministries that empower black youth to live in such a way that they are highly spiritual, academically successful, and authentically mission-minded, thus becoming productive contributors to society." —Carmichael Crutchfield, Assistant Professor of Christian Education and Youth Ministry, Memphis Theological Seminary, and General Secretary, Department of Christian Education, Christian Methodist Episcopal Church

JUDSON PRESS
PUBLISHERS SINCE 1824

YOUTH MINISTRY
IN THE BLACK CHURCH
Centered in Hope

Anne E. Streaty Wimberly

Sandra L. Barnes

Karma D. Johnson

JUDSON PRESS
PUBLISHERS SINCE 1824

Join our mailing list for updates and special offers.
www.judsonpress.com/mailing_list.cfm

Library of Congress Cataloging-in-Publication Data

Wimberly, Anne Streaty, 1936–
    Youth ministry in the black church : centered in hope / Anne E. Streaty Wimberly, Sandra L. Barnes, Karma D. Johnson. -- First edition
        pages cm
  ISBN 978-0-8170-1736-1 (pbk. : alk. paper) 1. Church work with African American youth. I. Barnes, Sandra L. II. Johnson, Karma D. III. Title.
    BV4468.2.A34W56 2013
    259'.2308996073—dc23

                                                            2013004149

To youth ministry leaders
whose call to ministry with black youth
and whose stories of hope sought and found in that ministry
inspired our desire to tell the stories and press on with hope
And to black youth
whose trials are real, yet who walk in hope
to become all that God desires

CONTENTS

ACKNOWLEDGMENTS

Preparation of this resource on youth ministry in the black church was set in motion by a research project we directed titled "Vision Quest: A Study of Efforts, Challenges, and Needs of Youth Ministry Leadership in Black Congregations." We entered the study with our own quest for hope for black youth through ministry with them. We could not have imagined the numbers who have joined us on this quest and proceeded with us through the completion of this resource. In the writing process, we were constantly reminded of hope sought and hope revealed by partners, guides, storytellers, and supporters along the way. Our hearts are full of joy and gratitude to overflowing because of the inspiration, wisdom, encouragement, and challenges they shared that made us press on to the finish line of the manuscript.

Surely another book could be filled if we were able to list every participant in the study along with numerous additional partners along the way. Yet we must not fail to mention and express appreciation to the group of youth ministry leaders, pastors, and youth in 833 churches across the country who gave freely of their personal stories and wisdom. This book became a reality because of their gifts of self, time, and denominational diversity. We also owe the book's contents to representatives in 31 of these churches who participated in the ethnographic study. This initiative was carried out by the skillful, caring help of two ethnographers, Dr. Richelle White and Rev. Adrienne Lotson. Much was also gained from the Vision

Quest Clusters in the Atlanta area under the leadership of Rev. Elizabeth Clements and Rev. Adrienne Lotson. And we stand in awe and gratitude for the soul stories shared, lessons learned, and hope declared from pastors, parents, and youth in New Orleans in the wake of Hurricane Katrina and Hurricane Rita.

Additional insights and encouragement were gratefully received from faculty representatives and students at five historically black seminaries, the Interdenominational Theological Center (ITC) in Atlanta, Georgia; Shaw Divinity School in Raleigh, North Carolina; Proctor School of Theology at Virginia Union University in Richmond, Virginia; Howard Divinity School at Howard University in Washington, D.C.; and Payne Theological Seminary in Wilberforce, Ohio. We also extend thanks for the spectacular leadership given by Rev. Adrienne Lotson, Rev. Byron Benton, Rev. Dr. Elenora Cushenberry, Minister Adlene Kufarimai, Deacon Ricci Young, and Brother Willie Williams in the youth ministry best practices workshop, as well as the performance by the Brooklyn, New York, Berean Baptist Church Drumline at the Vision Quest closing event.

Youth Ministry in the Black Church: Centered in Hope would not have happened without the help of those already mentioned. However, we shall forever remain grateful for Lilly Endowment, Inc., for their generosity in supporting the research efforts and the development of this resource. We also add heartfelt thanks and love to a group affectionately known to us as Sisters in the Spirit, who, with painstaking effort, read, commented on, edited, and proofed the manuscript. These sisters, who are executive staff members of the Youth Hope-Builders Academy (YHBA) of Interdenominational Theological Center (ITC), include Minister Pamela Perkins, Rev. Casina Washington, and Minister Sarah Poole Farmer. We also add our love and gratitude to Dr. Edward Wimberly and Dr. Richelle White for their roles as proofreaders and caring supporters in the manuscript preparation process. We offer our thanks, as well, to ITC for institutional resources given on behalf of the study and the completion of this resource.

Step Up and Imagine: Hope for Youth Ministry and Youth

For surely I know the plans I have for you, says
the LORD, *plans for your welfare and not for harm,*
to give you a future with hope.
—Jeremiah 29:11

"I am having the most exciting time of my life in my ministry with youth. But I must tell you that this ministry is also the most challenging of anything I have ever done. It's both exciting and challenging at the same time. Does that make sense? I mean, it keeps me on my toes! Of course, that's all right. I see what I do as important!"

These words of a youth ministry leader highlight the complex mix of what is real in youth ministry. They also punctuate the prevailing view of the essential nature of ministry with youth in today's black congregations. Making this ministry happen, however, is often challenging. We're encouraged and we see hope blossom when we're able to meet critical needs of our youth and succeed in reaching youth outside our congregation. We're ready to shout when more and more youth start coming around and some of our youth actually "get it," as evidenced by their living out the Christian lifestyle we want them to understand and practice. But let's be real. We hear it from other leaders, and there are times when we say it ourselves: "What should I do? Why am I failing? I try and try to do what I think is the right thing, but little or nothing seems to work!"

An Invitation to Step Up and Imagine

Place yourself here as a dreamer who dares to consider what is possible in the future for you, the youth ministry you lead, and other leaders. Allow yourself to reach beyond what is going on right now in your youth ministry and let your imagination loose to see in the future the most amazing ministry that flows from your mind and heart. What does it look like? What is your role? Who will it reach? How will you do it? What will happen to the youth and your congregation and our world because this amazing ministry has taken place?

Now reach into that vision and pull out an inspiring thought to put into place right now. Make the decision to do it and be ready to move openly into the different present it creates and, yes, even into the risk and challenge it presents. As you put your image from the future into the present, stop and consider: What in our own or another's ministry is already working? What are the jewels, or the "wow" of programs, practices, events, connections, attitudes, involvement, and commitments that we must not let go? Grab hold of those things! Surprising and creative happenings take shape when our quest for the future and the wisdom of the present and past connect.[1]

Claim hope for youth ministry and the youth you serve. Envision youth ministry possibilities by boldly entering a quest for an amazing unseen future while seeing with wide-open eyes where you are now and why. Read, think about, and decide what makes possible youth ministry in your church that shines as a living testament of God's plan for a future of hope for black youth.

We invite you to take a hard look at the trials and triumphs you've experienced in your youth ministry efforts. This invitation extends to leaders and others in the church, because responsibility for ministry with youth belongs to the whole "village." So, pastors, parents, those who prepare youth ministry leaders, and denominational leaders, you're invited to join in this endeavor of self-reflection to gain insights into youth ministry and to consider your present role in it—what you might do to inspire, guide, and sustain it. Know that it is more than the present that is at stake. The invitation is also to imagine all that is possible tomorrow and into the unseen future. Step up and claim hope for present and future ministry with black youth.

Support for Stepping Up

Throughout the pages of *Youth Ministry in the Black Church: Centered in Hope*, we will reflect on youth ministry where we are and connect with others through case illustrations, anecdotes, Scripture, strategies, church and youth program profiles, and best practices. Get connected further by joining with a colleague or a group to reflect on and decide the direction forward.

The material in the pages that follow draws from an extensive research undertaking called "Vision Quest: A Study of Efforts, Challenges, and Needs of Youth Ministry Leaders in Black Congregations." This effort was carried out through a national telephone survey of leaders of youth ministries in 833 black congregations across the U.S. and one in Bermuda, and spanned denominations, including African American Episcopal (AME), African American Episcopal Zion (AMEZ), various Baptist groups, Christian Methodist Episcopal (CME), Church of God in Christ (COGIC), Lutheran, Presbyterian, and United Methodist. Additional material in this resource comes from interviews with leaders and youth as well as observations of youth ministry activities in the ethnographic study carried out in thirty-one (31) churches selected from the telephone survey group.

Information from a smaller study of 247 churches in which seminary students were leaders or affiliates of youth ministries also contribute to this resource. These leaders were seminarians at five historically black seminaries including Howard Divinity School in Washington, DC; Interdenominational Theological Center (ITC) in Atlanta, Georgia; Payne Theological Seminary in Wilberforce, Ohio; Proctor School of Theology in Richmond, Virginia; and Shaw Divinity School in Raleigh, North Carolina. The resource also draws from narratives from numerous focus group meetings with youth ministry leaders, youth, and parents.[2] The study showed a many-sided picture of youth ministry that will give us some footing for our reflections. The study results will help us to look at three key overlapping areas in youth ministry (see fig. 0.1).

- Youth Ministry Leadership focuses on the vocation, qualities, preparation, and challenges of youth ministry leadership.

- Ministry with Youth centers on the varied triumphs and trials in building and sustaining ministry with youth.

- Congregational Support focuses on the ongoing support of pastors, parents, and members; adequate meeting spaces; and financial resources.

For a moment, sit in on a meeting with a group of youth ministry leaders. Consider where you are in the conversation. Who tells a story that resembles your story? What would you add to the dialogue?

Let Me Tell It: Stories of Triumph and Trial

In a meeting of youth ministry leaders in the national study, leaders freely told some of their experiences. Mary shared feelings of exhilaration resulting from a successful youth group lock-in. She said, "We had a good showing. And I'm happy to say that we had good support. Some of the parents really helped out. Well, it wasn't that easy getting the kids focused on, you know, the 'religious stuff'. They wanted to play and were into their cell phones—texting and stuff. But once we came to an agreement on tech times, we really got into Bible study and prayer time. Everybody was involved. They did some awesome skits that showed some deep thinking about decisions they would make as Christians even though the decisions might hinder their popularity with peers.

"Some youth volunteered and were great in leading praise, worship, and prayer. Everything's not easy in what we do with the kids. And I know there's a place for the tech stuff—but how and when best to use it is a big question. Do we really know what will reach them? No, I don't believe we always have it down pat. Do we even listen to them? I confess, not always. But we're trying—I'm trying—and some things like the lock-in help."

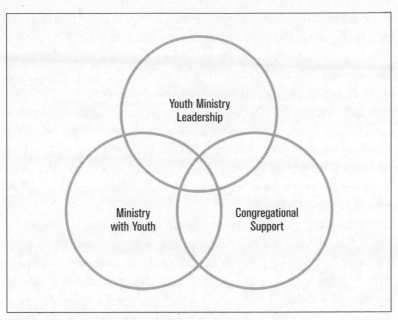

Figure 0.1. Areas of youth ministry.

Don interrupted, "But there is a problem. The way I see it, as leaders and churches, we have a hard time living, thinking, and breathing what our kids are living, thinking, and breathing. We don't speak or understand their jargon—hip-hop talk—or use the language in text messages or tweets. The truth is that texting or tweeting is new to some of us. There's also an underground culture that our kids belong to. If there's any hope, we've got to deal with the problem of being out of touch with that culture. It ain't about being cool or hip. It's about being relevant and able to be transparent and able to embrace and be embraced."

Diane called attention back to the lock-in: "I just wish we could get to something like a lock-in. It's almost like we're dying—I mean the youth ministry. The congregation has mostly older members who've been in the church most of their lives. They're used to doing things in a certain way, and I understand that. But we need to do something different if we expect the youth to come. Some of the members say they want a youth ministry because of all the youth in the neighborhood. But getting it done—well, outreach and support don't happen like they should. And the truth is that I'm a volunteer. We do have a small youth group, and I mentor several youth from the neighborhood. They say that church is not their thing. And truth be known, our youth are going through a lot today. They live in rough neighborhoods. Times are tough. Folks are poor. Families are hurting. Some of the youth are not in school and not working either. There's violence. Really, I don't know what to do."

From Kathy: "I feel ya. My situation is not exactly like that. But I agree—it's tough. In my church, the thing that has made a difference is the youth choir."

Fred added, "Yes. When we started a step group, we began to draw more youth. We're also fortunate to have resources to do a variety of things. Our youth are involved in community service. Youth Bible study is growing. We do a college tour for high school seniors. And Youth Sunday, where they are totally responsible for the service, has made a big difference. Letting them be leaders is important for them and the future of the church. Both the youth and the whole church need to come alive in a powerful way! At first there were some grumbles about the way the youth did things and their music. But it's working! Praise God!"

Mary made a final comment: "Let's face it. In too many cases, and in mine, what's happening with the youth just isn't the way I remember growing up. I agree with the earlier remark about today's generation. We have a hip-hop generation, a tech-centered generation, a troubled generation. It's not all bad—we see the promise too. I don't know about you all. Even though I'm doing my best, it's not enough! I'm tired! I mean, I got into this ministry 'cause God called me to it. But let's face it: it's hard. Sometimes I think I might need to move on. I also have a concern for the church. I hope something new will happen for the sake of our youth. I'm hoping for a different way, a good way forward."

Others nodded in agreement. One added, "You said it right. Hope? That *is* the way forward. If we're going to have a future, we've got to have it!"

Chart 0.1. A Beginning "Step Up" Reflection Guide

Triumphs	Trials	The Way Forward
Tell of a "wow" leadership accomplishment, program, activity, or event that made you feel good or proud and gave you hope.	Tell about leadership difficulty. • Tell of a time when you raised questions about your ministry calling. • Tell of a time when you either raised concerns about whether you had what it takes to lead or you needed more support for your leadership. • What other story would you tell of a sticky situation you faced in your role as leader?	Tell about the future. • What would you say is an amazing future for your leadership, program, activity, event accomplishment, and commitment? • What else would you add to your vision of an amazing future that involves your leadership?
Tell of some approaches you used that you would call "jewels" and are worth using again.	Tell of ministry disconnections with youth. • Tell of a time when you felt you weren't connected with youth culture. • Tell of a time when you felt you didn't have enough technology skills to keep the youths' interest. • Tell a story of a tough critical youth issue you found hard to address.	Tell where changes are needed to create an amazing future. • What would you say is a future that includes an amazing connection with youth? • Tell a story of your vision of uses of technology. • Tell a story of the most amazing way to help your youth deal with the toughest issue they are going to face in the future. • What else would you add to an amazing future of hopeful connections with youth?
Tell of the kinds of connections, attitudes, involvement, and commitments that brought about an increased youth participation. Think of a way you have already or will celebrate what happened.	Tell of disconnections with the congregation. • Tell of a time when you needed but did not receive sufficient congregational support. • What would you say about receiving parental or other adult support?	Tell about the future of congregational support. • How would you describe an amazing future of congregational support? Parental involvement? • Who would you describe as essential stepping partners? • What else would you add to an amazing future of hopeful support?

✓CHECK IT OUT

The leaders' stories are not unusual. Similar ones appeared in numerous meetings of leaders in the national study. Over and over they told of the pivotal role and numerous responsibilities of the youth ministry leader. They told of triumphs and celebration along with instances of trials. They mentioned the inescapable and sometimes difficult links between their leadership, youth programs and activities, congregational and parental support, financial resources, and space and time. Hope kept coming up. Hope came through as essential! Their stories are yours and mine. In preparation for stepping forward, get together with other youth workers and tell of some triumphs and trials you've faced and of your hope for the future. Use chart 0.1 to guide you.

Let's now step forward for further exploration, reflection, and imagining hope for youth ministry and our youth!

NOTES

1. Although their work applies specifically to the preparation of clergy, Foster and his colleagues make an important point that applies to the idea presented here about connecting past, present, and future as a practice of imagination. Their point is that pastoral imagination is all about a leader's or teacher's capacity to envision what is to be done in a pedagogical event by connecting vision for the future, discernment, tradition, and action. People begin to see themselves as agents of the future while pulling from tradition's story. See: Charles R. Foster, Lisa E. Dahill, Lawrence A. Golemon, and Barbara Wang Tolentino, *Educating Clergy: Teaching Practices and Pastoral Imagination* (San Francisco: Jossey-Bass, 2006), 40, 121.

2. Vision Quest was a three-year study sponsored by the Interdenominational Theological Center and underwritten by the Lilly Endowment, Inc. The purpose was to discover existing profiles of youth ministry leadership in black congregations as means of envisioning and making recommendations for youth ministry leadership that promotes the positive development of black youth. To ascertain the profiles, study efforts focused on roles and competencies of adults and youth who serve as leaders in church-sponsored youth ministries as well as on youth activities taking place in the church that were not church-sponsored. The study also focused on recruitment, the nature of youth served, the vision and expected outcomes of youth programs, preparation and support for leadership, challenges and needs, and approaches to addressing challenges.

INTRODUCTION
Steps to Hope-Centered Youth Ministry

*Surely there is a future, and
your hope will not be cut off.*
—Proverbs 23:18

Something about leaders taking on and carrying out youth ministry resembles a hip-hop dance routine. The popping and locking movements of hip-hop require every part of the body and every move to be in sync with the music. Making this happen is surely not easy. Yet trying to do it and arriving at points of accomplishment are what it's all about. Remembering to take time to rest from the long routines is important too. The word from a writer on hip-hop dance is that when the going gets tough and you wonder if you're going to make it, you just hang in there. You "turn on the music and hit the floor. Enjoy dancing to your heart's content; after all, dancing is all about celebration!"[1]

That's a word for all of us who are leaders in the multifaceted efforts of youth ministry. Amid the push and the pull of putting all the pieces together that make for a hope-filled youth ministry, we accept that hope leads the way. We step forward with our heart's content in celebration of the promise of our youth and in sync with what God has in store for them! But how do we do it? What are the steps we must take? What are the trials we face, and how may we overcome them?

Leaders across the country who were part of the Vision Quest study said that people need to be *called* to youth ministry leadership in order to step forward with hope in it. Our calling is our knowing that youth ministry is where we are supposed to be. In that calling, we're open to positive leadership experiences, opportunities, and support that appeal to and respond to youths' interests and needs. However, we will be tested, and questions about how best to reach, teach, and keep youth will stump us. After all, we are carrying out this ministry in an era of high-tech connections, youth culture changes, increased numbers of unchurched youth, and critical issues faced by youth and families. But there are steps forward we can take that include ideas of what to do and how best to do it as well as how to care for self amid vast investments of personal time and energy!

Leaders across the country also told of the necessity of taking steps that promote a congregational environment that says and keeps saying yes to youth ministry. Their word is that youth ministry thrives in a supportive "village" where pastors, parents, and other adults see youth ministry as a nonnegotiable endeavor. Regardless of size and location, congregations where youth ministry flourishes depend on youth ministry leaders *and congregations* stepping together to build and maintain hope-filled youth ministries. The question is, what does this 'stepping together' look like?

Our purpose in this introduction is to lay the groundwork for detailed answers that will come in the following chapters to questions about the steps necessary to enter into and carry out hope-centered youth ministry. Or, as hip-hop dance artists would say, our purpose is to prepare the floor to get to the rhythm and enjoy the beat.[2] In laying the groundwork, we offer these initial movements:

- Develop a set of convictions about the character of youth ministry leadership and youth ministry in your current and particular location.
- Consider the nature of hope you need.
- Be ready to claim hope.

Stepping Forward with Our Convictions

Convictions refer to unyielding beliefs we hold about the character of ministry with youth. Our convictions present a compelling snapshot of what we consider to be the nature of youth ministry or what we are convinced youth ministry ought to be about.[3] Leaders in the national study added another dimension. They told of the imperative of hope in youth ministry. When we insert hope at the center of our convictions, we infuse them with a specific kind of theological intention. Ministry scholars use the Greek word *telos* to name this intention.[4]

With the *telos* of hope in youth ministry, we highlight four things:

1. We affirm hope that drives our ongoing actions in youth ministry leadership and youth ministry. Hope centers on the promise that already exists in our youth and ministry with them, and it opens us to imagine what might yet be.[5]

2. Hope is what we see in our youth that we intend to build up and encourage *in* them.

3. Hope is the outcome that we want shown in the youths' claiming themselves and living as Christians unapologetically and black unashamedly.

4. Hope as the *telos* and at the center of our convictions means that we go about our ministry, knowing that "surely there is a future, and [our] hope will not be cut off" (Proverbs 23:18).

Consider the following three core convictions for hope-centered youth ministry that will receive more detailed attention later in this resource:

- Youth ministry leadership must be assured.
- Youth ministry practices must be relevant.
- "Village" support must be concretely experienced.

Conviction One: Hope-centered youth ministry leadership must be assured.

Hope-centered youth ministry is excellent youth ministry; and excellent youth ministry depends on excellent leaders. If we are serious about being a hope-centered leader, then we must be exceptional and first-rate in who we are as persons and what we do as persons in charge. Leaders, parents, and youth alike who participated in the national study made clear that people who take on and carry out ministry with youth must have some particular qualities and know-how. First, excellent leaders have a ministry that is *up close and personal*. We connect directly with youth and others by bringing our whole selves into ministry. The result is privileged relationships with youth and others connected with the ministry that require us to know who and Whose we are and what gifts we bring into the leadership role.

Youth ministry leadership brings us into up-close relationships with youth. Because our ministry has to do with the very lives our youth live, we need to know who they are, where they are, the concerns they have, and what makes them think and behave as they do. Moreover, to move with spiritual strength, we need an up-close relationship with God. In all we do as leaders, we need a connection with God in our daily prayer closets and access to other spiritual resources that help us stay focused on the example of Jesus Christ, maintain spiritual verve, and receive empowerment from the Holy Spirit to keep on keeping on. Vision and direction for youth ministry spring from a vital spiritual life.

Second, excellent youth ministry leadership happens because of the leader's *essential knowledge* of how to carry out the ministry. We may call it a leader's know-how that falls into two main categories: relational aptitude and operational aptitude. Excellent leadership depends on the leader's relational know-how to connect with youth, care for them, and not simply listen to them but learn from them and make way for their learning and leadership. We further exercise relational aptitude by what we do to celebrate our youth— their presence, their gifts, and their accomplishments.

But more than this, youth ministry relies on leaders' abilities to carry out relevant programs, activities, and evaluation. We do this through use of operational know-how. We may claim certain gifts for ourselves and the youth we serve, but youth ministry leadership comes alive only when we put these gifts into operation. Youth

Chart 0.2. A Short Introduction to Youth Leader Qualities

Knowing Ourselves, Our Youth, and Our Ministry as a God Thing	Putting Our Relational Aptitude into Practice	Putting Our Operational Aptitude into Practice
Know Ourselves • Our call • Our vision • Our personal qualities	**Connect with Youth** • Be available. • Get in touch with youths' needs. • Be a trusted mentor.	**Choose relevant programs and activities.** • Access parental and congregational support. • Access material and financial resources. • Engage in evaluation. • Decide how to move forward.
Know Our Youth • Who they are • Where they are • Their physical development • Their emotional development • Their cognitive development • Their environmental influences • Their social learning • Their cultural formation and awareness • Their spiritual development	**Collaborate with Youth** • Listen to youth. • Learn from youth. • Make way for youths' learning. • Make way for youths' leading.	
Know Our Ministry • Reliance on spiritual centering • Intent on prayer • Intent on self-reflection • Intent on spiritual disciplines	**Celebrate Youth** • Recognize their presence. • Honor their gifts. • Acknowledge their accomplishments.	

ministry comes alive as we recognize *who* is involved in it and *how* to do it. These two categories of knowing are summarized in chart 0.2 and will receive further attention below and in chapters 2 and 3.

Leaders strive for excellence in these areas in order for black youth to know themselves as Christians unapologetically and black unashamedly. We seek an outcome whereby black youth claim their Christian identity without feeling they must hide, deny, apologize, or make excuses for being Christian to their peers or anyone else.

Excellent leadership is also to lead to our youths' claiming fully and rightfully for themselves the words of the psalmist, "For you created my inmost being; you knit me together in my mother's womb. I praise you because I am fearfully and wonderfully made; your works are wonderful, I know that full well" (Psalm 139:13-14 NIV). Excellence is to assure that black youth not simply survive but thrive. How? In all that is done, the intent of youth ministry is to equip young people to think and act as valued, capable Christians who contribute in positive ways to the church and world both today and into the future. But for this to happen, it is essential to embrace an overarching view of youth and our ministry with them as blessings. In other words, it is critical that whatever we do in youth ministry, we have a sense of how God has gifted black youth, and we fully accept responsibility for nurturing them. This view builds on the biblical understanding that children are a gift of God (Psalm 127:3).

Hope-centered leaders enter the leadership role with an acknowledged call and commitment to it, and they have a vision for youth ministry that pivots on seeing and inspiring hope. Excellent leaders also prepare themselves to lead in the ways summarized in chart 0.2. But we recognize, too, that preparedness by itself is not enough. Inspiring hope happens because of our freedom to imagine what is possible, as well as our willingness to test out new ideas with others, including the youth, and to change up, or reframe, a program, experience, or activity based on that feedback. This kind of informed imagination reflects openness to the "new" based on evaluation of what has been, what is, and what might be. In this way, we as leaders become agents of hope whose vision takes seriously youth ministry as an unfolding journey.

✓ CHECK IT OUT

Consider the first conviction—hope-centered youth ministry leadership must be assured. How did you become involved in youth ministry leadership? Why is it important for you to be involved? What is your vision for youth ministry in your congregation? What does being an agent of hope in your ministry leadership mean to you?

Conviction Two: Hope-centered youth ministry practices must be relevant.

Chart 0.2 includes a reference to relevant programs and activities. Leaders in the study were up front in their assertion that relevance defines hope-centered youth ministry practices. Relevance refers to those activities that are outgrowths of *seeing* and *hearing* the youth with the goal of *reaching* them. Based on this preference for youth-focused ministry, relevance results from programs and activities undertaken with youth that are purposeful, have significance for them, and engender meaning and hope-building action in their lives.[6] But what constitutes relevant practices? Three overall keys will be explored here as a preface to a fuller discussion in upcoming chapters:

- Make affirmation and welcome of youth a priority.
- Be holistic in program offerings.
- Make certain of the intended impact of program activities on the youth.

The first key to relevant ministries with black youth begins with practices of affirmation and welcome. For black youth, knowing that they belong counts! Youth ministry practices with black youth center on countering perceptions of themselves as misfits in majority culture and outsiders in the congregation. A sense of self-affirmation and possibility for their unfolding lives builds when they experience both acceptance and affirmation as valued black human beings, each with his or her own distinctive characteristics and gifts. Vital ministry proceeds to experiences that emphasize the youths' holistic development as Christians and black persons. This means that ministry must address personal, relational, spiritual, cultural, educational, vocational, and situational aspects of their lives.

Beyond this, hope-centered youth ministry must also include practices that have an observable impact on the youth. As a transforming channel, hope-centered youth ministry is to contribute to black youths' meaning making; formation of character-building values, attitudes, skills, and positive identity; and development of resilient behaviors based on their understanding of the Christian faith. As a hope-centered endeavor, youth ministry builds in young people their ability to let go of negative life experiences and focus on the positive; to meet challenges successfully; to learn and apply new things; to develop social and communication skills; and to access resources. Desired outcomes can include spiritual formation, life skills development, cultural connection, and community awareness.

✓ CHECK IT OUT

Based on the conviction that hope-centered youth ministry practices must be relevant, consider the following: What does the youth ministry program include in your congregation? Why? How would you describe the participants in your youth ministry program? How did they become involved? What kinds of activities might the youth in your congregation and community suggest? Ask them for ideas. If you could "hope for" or "dream" a ministry with youth in your congregation, what would it be? Why?

Conviction Three: Hope-centered "village" support must be concretely experienced.

Our black forebears held to and acted on the African cultural adages "It takes a village to raise a child" and "I am because you are; and because you are, I am." For generations these pivotal communal views have reflected and engendered a culture of hope. And they are deemed by leaders in the national study to be more important today than they were in times past because of ongoing and new difficulties, pain, and struggle in our homes, schools, and communities.[7] The congregational environment that reaches into the community beyond the church matters more today than ever before. Parents and other adults in the lives of our youth, the congregation, and the larger community must offer support that matters.

A hope-centered village must be a present support for youth ministry in today's world of

- technology and social media;
- changing family configurations, including increasing numbers of single parents and of divorced and blended families;

- health and education disparities;
- disproportionate numbers of our young people in prison; and
- increasing numbers of unchurched youth.

Especially in light of these realities, being a hope-centered village means that our youth and ministry with them are central to a hope-building present and future of congregational and community life. A hope-centered village takes responsibility for providing concrete experiences with hospitable and safe ministry spaces; willing congregational partners; youth-centered technology; Afrocentric resources; church and community networking; and ongoing, stable, and competent leadership.

✓CHECK IT OUT

In response to the third conviction—hope-centered "village" support must be concretely experienced—think about the following: How would you describe the parents' and other adults' roles in your congregation's ministry with youth? What are the prevailing attitudes toward youth by members in your congregation? How does your congregation support ministry with youth? What are the most needed supports? If you could hope for ways for your congregation to be a better "village of hope" for black youth in and beyond your congregation, what would they be?

Stepping Forward with Hope

In developing our convictions about youth ministry leadership and ministry with black youth, we must keep hope central. Earlier we saw that hope gives us a theological intention or *telos*. It centers us on the promise already existing in our youth and ministry with them. It connects us to God's presence and activity and opens us to rely on God in our imagining what might yet be.[8] It connects us to God's promise of a future where hope will not be cut off (Proverbs 23:18).

For a moment, let's explore meanings of the kind of hope we want to claim in our ministry with youth. As a way of entering our exploration, we'll reframe the question sung by Tina Turner some years ago: "What's love got to do with it?" Our question is, what's hope got to do with youth ministry leadership and youth ministry? In answering the question, we will not give full details on what is involved in youth programs that build on hope. That will happen in forthcoming chapters. Instead, the intent is to draw our attention to how we think about hope and why we believe hope is important to what we do. Leaders in the national study were helpful in this regard. They pointed to four interconnected expressions of hope:

- mediating hope (2 Corinthians 5:14-20),
- shared hope or "village hope" (Proverbs 17:6; 1 Corinthians 12:12-26),
- transcendent hope (Jeremiah 29:11; 2; Hebrews 10:23), and
- critical evaluative hope (Proverbs 24:14; Philippians 3:12-14, 8-9).

The leaders described *mediating hope* as a practice of hope in our youth ministry leadership that requires us to be active agents or Christ's ambassadors of hope with and on behalf of youth. However, they added *village hope* as a necessity. This kind of hope is a village-centered hope that pastors, parents, and other adults in the congregation practice together. The leaders also spoke of *transcendent hope* that reveals God's presence and activity in and on behalf of our youth and all they and others do with them. This hope is a way of saying, "Without God we're not going to get very far." It is an overarching way of moving forward with hope. Finally, leaders said that we need *critical evaluative hope*. This particular kind of hope requires our willingness to honestly examine what we've done, what needs changing, and how best to continue on. The prologue suggested that we consider the "wow" of our programs, practices, events, connections, attitudes, involvement, and commitments that we must not let go. But we must also be ready to toss out anything that doesn't work and envision the possibilities for the future.

Let's explore more closely each one of these types of hope to get a bigger picture of what hope looks like, in advance of claiming it.

Mediating Hope

Mediating hope begins with the leaders. As youth ministry leaders, we are on the front lines of seeing where hope exists in and for today's youth and where it is yet needed. We are pivotal agents of hope—God's agents and ambassadors of Jesus Christ, who are about stimulating—mediating—a transforming vitality for life in our youth that helps them move through the promises and problems of life that will surely come. As agents of hope, we also stand with and on behalf of youth. We become aware of their struggles, know the present realities they face, stand with them, advocate for them, and provide spiritual and practical handles to build their faith and resilience. We hold on to an unwavering hope that, with God, they can make it in this thing called life. Consider the following conversation among youth ministry leaders:

Evelyn said, "The hope I see in the youth today is great. I think they really have great potential. They are very expressive and creative. The youth I see have determination and energy. Sure, they have a new way of expressing themselves and new ways of doing things in the 'wired world' we live in. I think it's up to us as leaders to find ways of helping them look critically at themselves. It's our responsibility to give them positive directions so the future looks fine for them."

Carter added, "You're right. There is hope if we step up to the plate. The truth is that we've got a lot of youth who are in school, in church, and are headed in a promising direction. But there are lots of areas across the country where we also find far too many dropouts, unchurched youth, gangs, teen pregnancy, all sorts of other health issues, and lots of incarceration. Too many of our youth see and live a negative story and somehow fail to see the promise. My point is that hope can happen only if and when we stand up with youth and for them."

Brent agreed. "There are a lot of kids out there who have a sense of being overwhelmed by circumstances and situations that they have no control over. There's a huge opportunity out there for us to make a difference. If we have hope for our youth, then we can't just be concerned about the youth in our churches. And whether they are in or out of our churches, we know all of them are going to live in the real world where things are tough. So we have to do something to help transform that reality. They can't do it by themselves. I see a lot of hope in our youth. And, I have a lot of hope for them. But they have a lot of hopelessness too. Like I said, we've got a huge opportunity. We need to take it!"

Audrey added, "I'm thinking of my generation. You know, we had aspirations when we were young. We used to dream. Well, I know myself, I dreamed, I hoped. I knew that one day I would become what I aspired to become. But I don't hear a lot of our youth having that dream, that aspiration, that strong will, that strong determination. Sure, not all of our youth have lost focus of what life is or what life can become in positive terms. But there is reason for concern for far too many, I think."

Connie chimed in: "My take on the question of hope is that it isn't where we were that counts. Whatever the case may be now is what we've got to address. We just have to take whatever is negative now and turn it into something positive. And we have to be sure that we know what negative means. Someone has already said that our youth are expressive and creative. I would add that our youth are smart. But not everybody sees it. And I'm not sure that our youth even claim it for themselves. Our youth and everybody else sees the media's uses of a broad brush to paint a negative picture of black youth. We want to make it possible for positive things to happen. We want them to see how they can do it too. But how it happens—it's on us!"

Carter concluded, "Our youth are our hope. When our hope is in them and for them, we have hope for ourselves. If we don't let them know of our hope and make a place for them and make good on it, very shortly the doors of our churches will probably close."

These youth ministry leaders give us several keys to forming the kind of *mediating hope* we need in youth ministry leadership:

- Mediating hope happens through leaders committed to be agents of hope that the apostle Paul calls ambassadors of Christ (2 Corinthians 5:20).

- Mediating hope does not happen in a vacuum. We form it with fullest awareness of the real stories of our youth, and we build ministries that help youth connect their stories to God's story, form Christian values and character, and make decisions based on their understanding of the Christian lifestyle.

- Through our embrace of mediating hope, we see God's possibilities for youths' lives and both envision and act on our own role on behalf of their seeing and acting on those same possibilities in spite of negative circumstances.[9]

- We apply mediating hope in a holistic youth ministry process that includes the aspects mentioned earlier and in the way we conduct ourselves as leaders. For leaders, this means demonstrating or putting into practice the implementing skills, essential attitudes, and vital values mentioned earlier.

- Mediating hope has an interdependent quality. This hope is directed toward our youth but is considered to be hope for us all.

Village Hope

Village hope, also known as *shared hope*, calls our attention to the congregation as a representation of God's family that extends beyond the walls of the church. In the earlier conversation of youth ministry leaders, Carter told of his awareness of unchurched youth. Some say connecting with them and getting the church to say yes to them is tough to pull off. But as youth ministry leaders, we and our congregations see youth both within and beyond the church's walls as our own. They are part of the village into which God has placed them. By expressing this communal vision and quality of hope, we show reverence for the value and giftedness of black youth with us and in the neighborhood around us that is given by God.

As tough as it may be, the village hope we believe in and act on means crafting in-reach ministry to in-church youth, outreach ministry to those beyond our walls, and full-reach ministry to keep youth once we get them. We find ways to invite, welcome, and minister in relevant ways to the extent that the church literally becomes a "church without walls." Chapters 7 and 9 show how to make this happen as well as ways of connecting village hope and mediating hope.

Village hope extends mediating hope by assuring human, financial, and location resources needed for vital ministry. As leaders, we may say, "This requirement is not new. In our particular case, it's also tough to do!" Congregations may also join in voicing difficulty. Yet leaders and congregations must keep it in the forefront and do whatever is possible to overcome the struggle. Why? Making this hope come alive means that leaders are not left to carry the ministry alone. Ministry with youth is to form leaders for the present and future church and world. It's about the whole community now and going forward. It takes the whole village—the leader, congregation, adults, and parents—to be active supporters to the end that they model endearing Christian values, emphasize the spirit of community, and cooperate with God's plan on behalf of a future with hope for youth (Jeremiah 29:11).

The essential need for making "village hope" a reality becomes magnified when we consider its absence. If leaders and congregations do not have this hope or fail to make it a reality, then leadership and youth ministry are doomed to fail and acquiesce to a foreclosed future for black youth. But if leaders, congregations, parents, and other adults together dare to embrace this hope and take its meaning seriously, then together they become communal agents of hope—Christ's ambassadors who assure the following:

- unmistakable affirmation of the youths' God-given value that mediates the youths' formation of hope in and for themselves;

- concrete ways of nurturing the youths' hope that result in their seeing themselves and those around them as valued creations of God;

- active involvement of youth and their unique gifts in the life of the church;

- youths' formation of spiritual values and resilience needed for living in a tough world in ways that honor, celebrate, and contribute to their own and others' well-being.

Transcendent Hope

Another view of hope expressed by leaders in the national study is transcendent hope. When leaders were asked how they entered into youth ministry, they often reported that it was God who called them. Moreover, when leaders shared stories of why they remained in this ministry in the throes of difficulties, limited support, and seemingly questionable outcomes, they told of receiving, as one leader put it, "inspiration from God, direction from Jesus, and energy from the Holy Spirit." Prayer to God was most often the means of regenerating hope in the midst of "not knowing what to do or whether to go on," said another leader.

The youth ministry leaders' conversation included a connection between hope, the presence and activity of God in the lives of the youth, and our role as leaders. In particular, Connie said, "If we're talking about hope, then it's up to us to re-present the picture with God's paintbrush of promise. Our job is to see the expressiveness, the creativity, and the intelligence that God has given youth and find ways to draw it out so that they are able to act with hope on their own and others' behalf." Connie's statement reminds us that when we center our hope in God and Jesus Christ, we acknowledge God as the ultimate source on whom we can rely in the nitty-gritty of our leadership. We realize that God is for us and the youth we serve and does not leave us alone in our leadership efforts.

God is not simply the one the leaders saw as the dependable source of all they hoped for in their ministry with youth, but God was the one whose reassuring presence appeared sometimes in surprising ways and just in the nick of time. In one youth ministry leader's story, hope had begun to wane as the result of the perceived inability to find the activities and approaches that resulted in what was deemed a successful, lively engagement of the youth. Moreover, attempts to get needed resources and more involvement of parents seemed to fail woefully. At nearly the brink of despair, the youth ministry leader reluctantly agreed to ask the youth for volunteers to speak at a church event at the initiation of the event committee chair. Several youth volunteered, much to the surprise of the leader. The presentations of the youth at the event brought tears to the leader's eyes. Each of the youth spoke about what it means to be a leader. They described the youth ministry leader as their model. They told about the inspiration they had received and the qualities they wanted for themselves.

As the result of this surprising outcome, the leader simply said, "God moves even when we feel stuck. That's the kind of God we serve." This experience gave the leader renewed hope and faith in God whose grace was affirmed by the apostle Paul in the words, "At an acceptable time I have listened to you, and on a day of salvation I have helped you" (2 Corinthians 6:2). The youth ministry leader's experience is a reminder that hope transcends what is occurring on a finite level in the present. The truth is that we cannot always see or know, really, how our ministry with youth will unfold or end even when we plan it to the nth degree. Hope means that we trust God who can be counted on.[10]

The point cannot be clearer! Transcendent hope is fundamental to what we do as leaders in today's ministry with black youth. The leaders in the national study give us some jewels or "wow" insights to remember. The foundation of our hope is God. Hope signals a belief in an open present and future where God is near and will not leave us alone. Even when we've reached our wits' end in trying out one thing and then another, God through Jesus Christ and the Holy Spirit opens the door to something new and gives us energy to keep on keeping on. One leader said, "I really believe hope means that we can trust God's guiding and sustaining what we do in our ministry. We can depend on God showing up to help us envision how to turn ineffective ministry around. It may not happen right away. And that's okay. The point is that we don't give up. We go on knowing that God did not give us a spirit of fear, but of power, love, and a sound mind (2 Timothy 1:7). A live future for our youth depends on it. A dynamic basis for action springs from it. Vision for ministry that addresses youth in the present builds on it."

Critical Evaluative Hope

We were surprised to learn that many leaders in the national study did not have plans or measures to evaluate what they were doing in youth ministry. But the cause and process of hoping demands our hearty critical reflection on all that brought us to our present place. When we evaluate our efforts, we consider what must be left behind and what will be the best way to go forward. Evaluation is all about asking and answering the questions raised in the prologue: "What should I do? Why am I failing?" It allows us to become the dreamer who dares to consider what is possible in the future for us, for the youth ministry we lead, and for the community in which our ministry takes place. When we anticipate reaching this point of dreaming as the result of our evaluation, we have not only grasped but also acted on a critical, evaluative hope.

Even though some leaders in the national study found it difficult to engage in evaluation, others did not. We learned from them that youth ministry in the present is connected consciously or unconsciously with previous endeavors. They told us that evaluation gave them several helpful perspectives. Acting on evaluative hope lets us know that we should do the following:

- Continue some things we did in the past because they work for us now. We call this the *continuity of practices.*

- Let go of some things because they were good for a previous time but out-of-date or inappropriate for the present. We call these *practices of disallowance.*

- Be aware of needed ministry actions that failed to materialize; and on this basis, look for opportunities to put them in place. These are *practices of allowance.*

- Embark on new ways of doing things in new and specific circumstances (for example, changes in technology, family structures, youth culture, crises). These are *practices of change.*

- Be aware of the ministry of predecessors and preconceived notions of congregations in situations where youth ministry leadership and/or youth ministry is new. What to do next must emerge out of intentional and critical evaluation of what has already been considered or effected. We practice *connecting with the past.*

When we take seriously all of these dimensions of evaluative hope, we not only step up to connect the past and present and to imagine a promising future, but we discover a ministry plot— where we are headed and whether we are moving wisely and with hope or need to regroup. This is part of the hoping process.

✓ CHECK IT OUT

In response to the various steps to hoping, ask yourself the following questions: What hope do I see in today's black youth? What story would I tell that paints a picture of this hope? What is the hope that youth I know have for their lives? Why is my hope for the youth and their hope for themselves important? What struggles with hope for our youth do I have? Where do I either see or seek God's presence and activity in my youth ministry leadership or in my congregation's role in it?

The Direction Forward

The chapters that follow invite us to explore in fuller detail the nature, processes, and practices of hope-centered youth ministry in the black church. Building on the convictions and meanings of hope appearing in this introduction, the chapters invite us to explore the characteristics of hope-centered youth ministry leadership, key processes and best practices of hope-centered ministry with black youth, and strategies for building hope-centered youth support. The detailed information appearing in the chapters draws from the wealth of data gained in the national study and is enhanced by illustrative material in the form of stories, anecdotes, Scripture, strategies, and church and youth program profiles. Through uses of illustrative material and questions, the book invites personal reflection and thus functions as a participatory resource. We have organized the book in three parts.

Part 1 answers the question "How do we assure hope-centered youth ministry leadership?" Building on the overall theme of Hope-Centered Youth Ministry Leadership, this opening section of the book includes four chapters. Chapter 1, "Called to Lead:

Who, Me? Why Me?" tells us that hope-centered youth ministry leadership happens when we acknowledge, accept, and stay in touch with our calling to it. It invites us to remember and retell our call story and to reflect on its meaning for us today. Using real-life stories, the chapter includes varied ways persons enter youth ministry leadership, such as spiritual callings received during adolescence and nontraditional paths to vocation, including the desire to give back, being pressed or driven into leadership, or recognizing a passion and gift for it. The chapter then invites us to explore our ministry vision, based on the view that leaders are called or summoned, even commanded by God *to* something. This part of the chapter builds on vision statements given by youth ministry leaders in the national study.

The title "Leading with Hope: Up Close and Personal" frames chapter 2. This chapter invites leaders to explore what of our personhood we bring into the leadership role. Attention is given to motivation and personal qualities, including nine signature qualities identified by leaders and youth in the Vision Quest project as important to excellent youth ministry leadership. The chapter goes on to detail adolescent developmental characteristics and distinctive concerns of black youth. Emphasis on the leader's spiritual centeredness, reliance on God, and uses of spiritual resources follow, as well as a closing reflection guide for leaders to use individually or in a group.

Chapter 3 is titled "Growing as Hope-Centered Leaders." Key how-tos of making youth ministry come alive are included in this chapter. Specifically, the chapter describes four pivotal relational capacities or the kind of relational aptitude leaders should exhibit, including connecting, caring, collaborating, and celebrating. It continues with necessary operational skills, or the operational aptitude required for choosing, developing, and managing programs and activities and approaches to program evaluation that lead to decisions about the ministry's onward movement.

Chapter 4 addresses the imperative for preparation for youth ministry leadership. Called "Preparing for Hope-Centered Leadership," the chapter explores why leadership preparation is necessary.

Informed by the national study of youth ministry leadership, the chapter provides a range of formal and informal pathways to preparation and kinds of encouragement needed for leaders to maintain preparedness along the ministry journey regardless of gender, age, leadership type, church size, or denomination. The chapter openly presents challenges faced by leaders, many of whom are unpaid volunteers. Case examples expose the cry of leaders for help in hope-draining environments and offer concrete, usable individual and pastoral support practices that can equip leaders. A set of scriptural, hope-centeredness steps based on Jesus' model of staying in touch with what it means to prepare and pay attention to ongoing preparedness conclude the chapter.

Part 2 addresses the theme "Hope-Centered Youth Ministry" and answers the question "What actions and activities make youth ministry come alive for black youth?" This section gives attention to ways of building a "culture of hope" that affirms and welcomes youth and "contents of hope" that include vital, youth-friendly, and holistic program offerings. The three chapters in Part 2 feature best practices that have a positive impact on youth.

Titled "Welcome Matters: Seeing, Reaching, and Hearing Youth," chapter 5 utilizes stories from varied congregational and youth ministry workshop settings to explore processes of *seeing*, *reaching*, and *hearing* black youth; how the three dynamics differ; and the commitment and intentionality needed by youth ministry leaders to make all three happen. The chapter assumes that our seeing, reaching, and hearing youth are distinct activities of hospitality that are needed to build a culture of hope and therefore describes each one in detail. Importantly, the chapter responds to the historic generational tendency for black youth to be seen but not heard. It suggests ways of giving voice to black youth and using their stories and thoughts to prepare, implement, and evaluate hope-centered ministry with them. We provide a chart for setting youth ministry goals that take seriously the real stories youth live everyday and that lead to relevant programs and activities for them. Moreover, the chapter provides concrete suggestions for achieving ministry goals. Because communication is key in achieving authentic hospitality, concrete tips on how to hear youth, reach out to them, and welcome them appear in this chapter.

Chapter 6, "Making Tech Connections: Youth Ministry in a High-Tech World," highlights the new age of widening techno-communication options that require creative ways of promoting youth involvement and engaging them in vital ministry. Drawing on the national study data, the chapter presents pros and cons of congregations' incorporation of technology in youth ministry and provides steps to help youth ministry leaders choose and gradually build from a variety of options. The chapter gives attention to the less common but exemplary churches that use youth-centered technology such as websites, Facebook, chat rooms, Twitter, and podcasts to attract and retain youth.

As the final chapter in Part 2, chapter 7, "Real Hope: Programs of Promise," uses national survey findings, stories of youth ministry leaders, and firsthand observations of programs and settings in which youth ministry takes place. This final chapter documents best practices that are based on youth ministry goals and contribute to hope-centered youth ministry. It gives special attention to Afrocentric practices and resources; gender-focused, arts-centered, and issues-focused best practices; responses to catastrophic events such as Hurricane Katrina; church and community networking; resources for ongoing, stable youth ministry leadership; and youth group renaming.

In light of the crucial need for congregational support of youth ministry with black youth, Part 3 provides detailed responses to the question "What constitutes hope-centered village support?" Using the theme "Hope-Centered Youth Ministry Support," this final section of the resource includes two chapters. Chapter 8, "Parent Power: Parents as Hope-Builders," presents varied forms of parental involvement in youth ministry with the intent of fostering needed ministry support and opening pathways of communication between parents and youth that perhaps did not exist before. Building on stories of actual parents, the chapter provides examples of how partnering with parents can occur. It also provides foundational principles highlighting the importance of generational connections and discusses the commonalities and differences across generations. This chapter also gives specific ways to invite parents to envision their roles through shared stories. The chapter closes with an action plan worksheet for parents' involvement.

Chapter 9 is titled "Village Power: The Congregation as Hope-Builder." This chapter asserts that a vitally interested and committed congregation is needed to assure hope-centered ministry with black youth. We draw on concrete examples of a congregation's relational aptitude and operational aptitude, giving special attention to the nature and importance of teamwork, to show the qualities of a hope-building culture in which youth ministry triumphs. We also include a guide to assess features of a village of hope that promote triumphant youth ministry and aid youth ministry in trouble. The chapter ends with a checklist for congregations to determine necessary hope-building actions.

The closing section of this interactive resource is an epilogue titled "Claiming Hope, Moving Forward." Readers are invited to reflect on what it means to claim hope in ministry with black youth. We invite youth ministry leaders and all who are part of youth ministry to claim hope by reaching out to receive and welcome youth; attest to the certainty of what we receive; accept what we receive as gift; become responsible agents of hope; celebrate the blessings that come from youth ministry; recognize the Source of the gift; and commit to a village dance that inspires movement forward.

NOTES

1. Gaurav Shimpi, "Hip Hop Dance Routines," Buzzle.com, 2, http://www.buzzle.com/articles/hip-hop-dance-routines.html, accessed July 6, 2012.

2. Ibid., 1.

3. Jerry H. Stone, "Narrative Theology and Religious Education," 255–85, in Randolph Crump Miller, ed., *Theologies of Religious Education* (Birmingham, AL: Religious Education Press, 1995), 268. Stone describes convictions from the perspective of their importance to what is embodied in the biographical narratives of figures chosen for use in Christian education. But the description is useful for our discussion of youth ministry in that it highlights the beliefs or moral principles on which convictions center.

4. An example of the use of *telos* appears in James K. A. Smith, *Desiring the*

Kingdom: Worship, Worldview and Cultural Formation (Grand Rapids: Baker, 2009), 54. Smith says that love stands as the *telos*, or way of describing, what is central to people's "hoped for, longed for, dreamed of picture of the good life." This love is directed toward the kingdom of God.

5. Anne Wimberly argues that fostering a future of hope is the *telos*, or direction, for both our relationships with youth and ministries with them. See Anne E. Streaty Wimberly, "Leaders' Perspectives on Youth and Youth Ministry: Insights and Discoveries," Resources for American Christianity, http://www.resourcingchristianity.org, 13, accessed September 23, 2012.

6. This view of practices reflects, in part, the description given by Craig Dykstra, *Growing in the Life of Faith: Education and Christian Practices*, 2nd ed. (Louisville: Westminster John Knox, 2005), 69–70. Dykstra describes practices as "those cooperative human activities through which we as individuals and as communities, grow and develop in moral character and substance. . . . They are ways of doing things together in which and through which human life is given direction, meaning, and significance and through which our very capacities to do good things well are increased."

7. Robert M. Franklin writes in *Crisis in the Village: Restoring Hope in African American Communities* (Minneapolis: Fortress Press, 2007), 24, about a definable crisis in the community-wide village that requires a "village renewal process" because of the failure of leaders to coordinate, sequence, fund, and revise efforts on behalf of a more hopeful future for our children.

8. Anne Wimberly, in "Leaders' Perspectives on Youth and Youth Ministry," 13, argues that fostering a future of hope is the *telos*, or direction, for both our relationships with youth and ministries with them.

9. In a sense, this view of mediating hope bears some kinship to the "emancipatory hope" set forth by Evelyn Parker in *Trouble Don't Last Always: Emancipatory Hope Among African American Adolescents* (Cleveland, OH: Pilgrim, 1993). However, mediating hope differs from Parker's central focus on the nature and formation of leadership of teens and adults for the express purpose of dismantling oppressive structures by freeing their ability to engage in transformative action. *Mediating hope* reflects a broader, more holistic youth ministry process.

10. This view of hope may be further enhanced by the fuller exploration of a theology of hope discussed in Andrew Lester, *Hope in Pastoral Care and Counseling* (Louisville: Westminster John Knox, 1995), 59–71.

PART 1

Hope-Centered Youth Ministry Leadership

Therefore prepare your minds for action;
discipline yourselves; set all your hope
on the grace that Jesus Christ
will bring you when he is revealed.
—1 Peter 1:13

1
CALLED TO LEAD
Who, Me? Why Me?

*I pray that the God of our Lord Jesus Christ,
the God of glory, may give you a Spirit of wisdom and
revelation as you come to know God, so that, with the eyes
of your heart enlightened, you may know what is the hope
to which God has called you, what are the riches of God's
glorious inheritance among the saints, and what is the
immeasurable greatness of God's power for us who believe.
—Ephesians 1:17-19*

Let's be honest—leading youth can be scary! We often have a lot of responsibility, limited resources, and more complaints than compliments. Our roles can seem even scarier when we think about the impressionable young lives in our hands. So, given its many challenges, why do we do it? What answer would you give to the question "How and why did you get involved in youth ministry leadership?" Some leaders like Edna have a "Here am I, send me" experience. Several youth ministry leaders gave responses like hers: "I know God has called me to make a difference in the lives of young people. I have this burden that God put deep inside me that this is what I must do. And it seems that along the way, God has placed me where youth are to remind me of my calling."

Ray, another called youth leader, said, "I'm convinced that youth ministry isn't for everybody. You have to be called to it! I know I'm called. But sometimes I find myself sitting in a corner somewhere talking to myself, saying, 'Called? Me? Why me?' Let's face it. The truth is the demands are great. So are the responsibilities. You've got to be 'on it' 200 percent. It's tough stuff! But then, great stuff happens too! In the thick of things, God gives the increase.[1] So my answer to my own question always comes out, 'Why not me?' I confess again that I was called to this ministry. Or, to be more to the point, God chose me for it!"

Although youth ministry leaders from across the country who participated in the Vision Quest study gave many reasons for their involvement in youth ministry, most said they had not thought about their call to youth ministry for a long time. Some had never shared their call stories. But in the process of sharing, they were reminded that they are where they are for a reason. But more than this, telling our call stories brings us face-to-face anew with the questions "What's my reason for being a youth ministry leader *now*?" and "What does God want of me and the ministry with youth I am in?"[2]

These questions point to a connection between our call to youth ministry leadership and our vision for youth ministry. We are not simply called. We are called *to* something. Making this connection is important, because it is not unusual for a vision or "picture" of youth ministry to accompany our call. For example, one leader described being called to serve inner-city youth by engaging them in a rites of passage program. When our vision comes alive, as it did for this leader, we experience a congruency between our call and our vision. We say, "I'm where I'm supposed to be. I'm doing what I'm supposed to be doing." It just feels right.

Sometimes, however, the vision of ministry we hope for and what is actually occurring do not coincide. In this case, remembering our call can rekindle our passion or reframe our ministry with youth. One leader responding to our study remembered how several youth testified about overcoming difficult circumstances because of his care. Because of these testimonies, he experienced a renewed surety of his call that had begun to wane in a season of seemingly unending challenges. Another leader recalled struggling with what seemed an unsuccessful ministry. As she retold the story of her call, she said, "It's not the ministry that's the problem. It's me. There's another way to move. I see it now."

As indicated in the prologue, our era of rapid change, technological advancement, and multiple challenges faced by black youth has resulted in more and more stories of leaders grappling with how best to carry out youth ministry. They grapple with how to move from their call to a vital vision for youth ministry. The question becomes not simply "Who, me? Why me?" but "Where does hope lie in what I do?" Leaders realize they cannot ignore changes that affect the present and future of youth ministry. The requirements of remembering their call, reframing ministry, and reframing hope come forth. They realize the need to discern the new while building on the best from past efforts.[3]

In this chapter, we invite you to tell or retell your call stories alone, with a colleague, or in a group with other leaders. You are invited to experience "evocative moments" that trigger reflections of why you are in youth ministry leadership. The intent is to make you think about where you've been, where you are now, and where you're headed. Returning to your call is meant to get you in touch with that "spark," that energy, and that excitement that may need to be rekindled inside you for your ministry journey forward.

For some, the process of remembering will beckon you to sit for a while and answer the question that has surfaced from time to time: "Called to lead. Who, me? Why me?" In addition, because of the connection between call and vision, this chapter also invites you to consider both in light of present realities. To guide your recalling and reflection, we provide a range of types of calls to youth ministry leadership followed by real-life call stories. We then move to the nature of our vision for youth ministry, using real-life stories as sources for reflection. And finally, we present opportunities for individual response, reflection with a ministry partner, or group discussion.

Remembering the Call to Youth Ministry Leadership

Simply put, a calling typically refers to our awareness that God is directing us into some form of Christian ministry. While reflecting, persons often pinpoint the nature and circumstances of the call experience and the ministry to which they are called.[4] Youth ministry leadership happens because we are "called" in some manner to it. Statements such as Edna's and Ray's, for example, highlight that the call sometimes comes in a discernible voice of God—*God's call* (see chart 1.1). Their comments are a reminder that some of us were probably told by a family member, pastor, or friend, "You're going to be a pastor," or "You have the gift of relating with youth. You need to 'go for it.'" Our embrace of this *prophesied call* moved us down a pathway into youth ministry leadership.

Others developed a deeply felt passion to work with youth because of mentors who modeled the Christian lifestyle before us and helped us get through adolescence. This *call to give back* became the motivation for youth ministry leadership. For still others of us, youth ministry leadership became connected or added to other responsibilities. We experienced this *call to enhanced service* when our role as pastor extended to that of youth ministry leader, or when we volunteered as a layperson beyond our full-time secular vocation. And, yes, there are those who have been *pressed into service* by a call from a church official: "Help! We need you!" Or, we considered the call as a nonnegotiable demand from a committee or from within ourselves to create a ministry where none existed. At times, response to a particular call was gradual because of a reluctance to "step up" to the demand—"I'm not ready for this." Then the thought came, "Hmm, this youth ministry leadership thing may be something I ought to consider." And then, "I really want to do it." Moreover, youth ministry leaders who are parents remind us that a special *parental call* came as an appropriate and welcome one to assure adolescent children's growth in the Christian faith and involvement in congregational life. And still some leaders describe a call experience that differs from the six categories described above.

With which calling(s) do you resonate, keeping in mind that more than one is possible? What calling have you had that is not included? In chart 1.1, check the callings that apply to you. Add a category that is not included if necessary. Consider the call stories in Scripture for added insights.

The type of call that draws leaders into youth ministry does not stand alone. Identifying it is one part of sharing a whole story in what invariably becomes "a sacred moment," as Edna said, "when I feel like I'm being called anew." While reading the upcoming stories, we are invited to remember our whole stories and the meanings they hold for us today.

Call Stories

God's Call

Delphine said, "It just seemed like God was calling me to a ministry with youth from the time I was a youth myself. My peers would always come to me for advice. They relied on me. I didn't mind being in that role, but I didn't connect it to any future ministry until, during a youth Sunday at church, the pastor invited all of the youth

Chart 1.1. Identifying the Call to Youth Ministry Leadership

Calls Come in Various Ways. What Was Your Call?	Mark All That Apply	Reflect on Scripture
God's Call. God spoke to me and called me.		**Joshua's Call:** Joshua 1:1-9 **Jeremiah's Call:** Jeremiah 1:4-8
Prophesied Call. Someone prophesied that God's plan was for my leadership.		**Samuel's Call:** 1 Samuel 2:18-21; 3:1-19
Called to Give Back. I was called to guide youth because of others' guidance of me.		**Lydia's Call:** Acts 16:11-15, 40
Called to Enhanced Ministry. I was called to be pastor and youth minister. Or I was called as lay volunteer leader beyond my full-time vocation.		**David's Call and Roles:** 1 Samuel 16:14-23; 17:1-50; 20:1–24:20 **Deborah's Call:** Judges 4–5.
Pressed into Ministry Call. I responded to a cry for help, or what seemed like a nonnegotiable demand or need.		**Jonah's Call:** Jonah 1:17–2:10
Parental Call. I stepped into leadership to assure my children's growth and involvement in congregational life.		**Call to Parents:** Deuteronomy 6:4-9; Psalm 78:1-7; 1 Timothy 1:1-7
Other. Identify your call that differs from the above.		

to come to the altar. I remember hearing the pastor say that God has a plan for each one of us. At that moment I really heard God speaking to me and saying, 'Look at what you're doing now with your friends. I'm preparing you for what you will do in the future.' Of course, the truth is, when I got my calling, I rejected it. Just because I was called by God didn't mean I answered. I wrestled with my call. But, although I was not answering my call, God was still sending me through things. Like, in college, the jobs that seemed to come to me were with youth. I worked in youth camps during the summer. I became an assistant in the college chaplain's office. I finally came to my senses when the chaplain asked me if I had ever thought of going to seminary. That was the turning point. I took things very, very seriously, moved in that direction, and guess what? It's all history now. I've been youth pastor for several years. Oh my God, I'm blessed. I am blessed, so I just thank God."

Prophesied Call

Barbara, a seminarian, told of wrestling with her calling even though others had seen it. She said, "It wasn't like some people [who] talk about their calling at twelve or thirteen years old when God hit and 'knocked them dead.' . . . It was like God had been calling me all of my life through others who knew me. I finally opened my ears and heard it. I wasn't sure where I was headed. I knew becoming a pastor of a church was part of my call. I went to seminary with that in mind. As part of my seminary journey, I was asked to take on the youth program in a local congregation. I enjoyed it. I was told by the pastor and others in the church that youth needed people like me who had a heart for them. My call became clearer. Youth ministry became a part of how I responded to that call."

Similarly, a family member's disclosure of her certainty that Barry would become a minister became part of his unfolding call story. His family member's prophecy became reframed into his commitment to youth ministry. He said, "Before I was born, my grandmother told my mother that I would be a minister. As soon as I was born, I began to be raised in a way that would make that prophecy come true. So, as a little kid, I knew what I was going to be when I grew up. I rebelled against it in my teen years. But it never fully left me. Also, I come from a family of educators. In this family, I grew up with an understanding that you have to invest in the lives of others, especially young people whose opportunities may well depend on what you do on their behalf. Without really realizing it, I was brought up with the expectation that you reach out and reach back to young people because of the importance this may have for their future. I actually started out as an educator, and I loved it! Then I was called to seminary. I held on to that earlier expectation. So it's kind of always been part of me and remains with me now in my leadership of young people. The youth stuff is the most fulfilling."

Call to Give Back

Now in his late thirties, Bernard began his call story by telling of his participation in Sunday school and youth ministry during his adolescence. "Attendance at Sunday school and youth programs enabled me to have a real interest in the work of the church. . . . When I was fourteen, in our little church, I was made church school superintendent. . . . At seventeen I felt God's call to ministry. My dad was my pastor. He and the leaders of the church gave me many opportunities to develop my gift of leadership. They poured into me what they knew. They encouraged me. They helped me to feel the pull of God's hand in my life. I have made youth ministry central throughout my years because I needed to give to youth what had been given to me. Just as it had been with me, I know that youth need the church in terms of Christian formation [which is] to have Christ formed in them . . . and to realize that they have essential worth, dignity, and sacredness. . . . Christian formation is needed so that youth can begin to feel the pull of the hand of God on their lives, and [can] begin to have a sense of being called or drawn to what God is trying to do in the world; and this means being led to give their lives meaning and purpose and direction in Christian vocation. So, in short, I have thought that in my ministry, I needed to respond to God's call on my life by giving back through work with youth that enables that sort of thing to happen."

Call to Enhanced Ministry

Although called expressly to pastoral ministry, Angela said that she had been a youth ministry leader since her teen years. She told of being "at home" in that role, of knowing what it entailed and demanded. She said, "I fell in love with it. But God called me to be a pastor, and I went to seminary to prepare for that responsibility. After seminary my calling was fulfilled by my appointment to a church. But guess what? God has a sense of humor, because there was no youth ministry leader in that church. There was no youth ministry to speak of. I knew it was up to me to get that ministry started. My role as pastor was quickly modified as I became the head of youth ministry as well."

Jeff also told of starting youth leadership when he was a youth. He said that as a result, "it was just normal for me to serve in that way." However, he told of hearing a sermon during his teen years that spoke directly to him. "The Holy Spirit was all over me, and I knew that God was calling me to preach. . . . I told my youth leader about it; and as she had asked, I gave my testimony to the youth group. I've been preaching from that time on. However, the truth is that I didn't give up on leading youth. Even after seminary, I knew that God still had something for me to do with the youth—that youth ministry is where God would have me be prior to taking a senior pastor position."

Anna described herself as a layperson who "didn't really know anything about a call, but found myself involved with the youth and liking it. There wasn't anybody else around to do it. Even though my everyday job is demanding, I couldn't say no to my heart. Well, if that's what a call means, then sure, I guess I was called."

Pressed into Youth Ministry Leadership

Stories abound of leaders, typically laywomen, who tell of receiving a literal telephone call from a pastor or church official who said, "I need your help with the youth!" (which often sounded like God's summons to Jonah: "I'm calling you to come to Nineveh!"). Similar stories reveal youth ministry leaders who were pressed into service because of their background in leadership, as in Amy's case.

"Because I had been a teen counselor in the school district, I was seen as the best person to chaperone a number of kids on a camping trip. Honestly, I didn't want to do it, and I was reluctant to agree. Finally, I said, okay, you've got me. Actually, it became an open door for me to become involved with youth in a new way. . . . It was an unpaid learning experience and a good one. . . . I grew into the role of youth ministry leader at my church. The point became clear to me that our youth in the church, just like adults in our church, have needs to be met and that they are not second-class members. They are able to learn the Christian faith and to strive to live the faith just as long as someone gives them that push or that caring or that assistance they need to get through their days as youth."

Parental Call to Lead My Children's Youth Group

A prevailing observation is that today's parents are not always involved in ministry with their adolescent children. Yet some parents remind us that the picture of parental involvement should not be painted with a single brushstroke. This view was adamantly shared by Deanna, who began as a volunteer on a youth ministry leadership team when her daughters were in their teen years. She said, "I have a vested interest in what goes on. I want the best for my children and the other children too. We have to be more than bystanders. Of course, I don't want to get in the way either. Actually, in our situation, a group of parents play a significant role in supporting the youth ministry team in whatever way possible, whether it's helping to lead small-group sessions, bringing food for and preparing cookouts, chaperoning at lock-ins or community service events, or providing 'shuttle service.' I feel like we as parents must not be invisible. I'm committed to being a part of the leadership team as long as my youth are in the youth group."

Consider Sharing Your Call Story

Youth ministry leaders are quick to say that sharing their call stories has a special impact on them. There is a sense that hearing themselves speak the story aloud affirms their needed staying power in leadership. It helps them hang in there! Indeed, out of the experiences of self-revealed call stories have come what may be termed the "four C's of keeping on keeping on."[5] More specifically, remembering and sharing the call keeps youth ministry leaders:

- *centered on the one who calls.* When I hear myself say, "God called me," there is no confusion about what I'm supposed to do. I can't deny that call. I must go on.

- *conscious of the road ahead.* When I was called, God gave me an idea of what this ministry should be about. It's about the youth! No, there's not always a clear picture of how best to make it happen. But the call keeps me open to the options and ready to see the vision as it unfolds.

- *courageous in the line of fire.* Ministry with youth today is hard. Nobody can tell me otherwise. But cowardice is not the answer. Remembering my call gives me the nerve to go on. President Obama called it "the audacity of hope."

- *committed to make a difference.* My call reminds me that I have a responsibility to be present to and to stand by our youth no matter what. Their very lives depend on leaders committed to go the distance with them for the sake of the gospel of Jesus Christ made real in their lives and lived through them. For that reason, I am compelled to continue on.

✓CHECK IT OUT

Based on the foregoing stories of the call to youth ministry leadership and the impact of sharing our call stories, you are invited to revisit your call story. Find a quiet space for personal remembering or enter into an "inquiry space" with a colleague or group of youth ministry leaders. Respond to the following: What personal story would you tell of how you became involved in youth ministry leadership? When and where did you know youth ministry leadership was going to be your vocational direction? Who was instrumental in your movement in that direction? Why was it so important for you to become involved in ministry with youth? How does your call story relate to your current involvement in youth ministry leadership? What new thoughts about youth ministry leadership come to mind?

Vision of Ministry with Youth

Consider again the earlier statement that we are not simply called—we are called or summoned, even commanded, by God *to* something. "To something" refers to a vocation of serving youth either in a full-time capacity or as a volunteer apart from or in conjunction with other congregational or secular work responsibilities. And our calling nudges us toward a particular vision or image of youth ministry that surfaces at the intersection of our calling and awareness of the needs and desires of youth. But most importantly, it comes into view as we discern God's intention for our ministry with youth. One leader put it this way: "Hope-filled youth ministry leadership happens when a leader has 'had a little talk with Jesus,' and is given a vision from the Almighty to guide the youth God sends."

Vision has to do with what God desires to happen through our ministry that will make the gospel of Jesus Christ become real in the lives of our youth. A vision for youth ministry is an aspiration or target toward which this ministry aims. Upon entering the ministry to which we have been called, the vision may serve as an anchor for building a youth ministry. It may also function as a stimulus for congregational action. It is a specific way of imagining the ministry with youth into which our calling is taking us.

We must be aware, however, that after starting out with the vision that emerged from our call, our vision may change along the way as we become knowledgeable about our ministry context, receive feedback from others, or discover particular needs and opportunities. Our vision and how it unfolds is not simply up to us. God does not simply call us and give us a vision. God speaks and gives glimpses of the way forward to others and creates definable points in time, what have been called *kairos* moments, for pictures of the future to take shape. For this reason, new awareness in the throes of youth ministry of God's activity may occasion the revision of our vision. Indeed, we may discern something new in our call. Certainly, with regard to vision, we aren't dreaming an impossible dream; we are dreaming what is most possible. Because our vision needs to be realistic, it requires knowing the facts and understand-

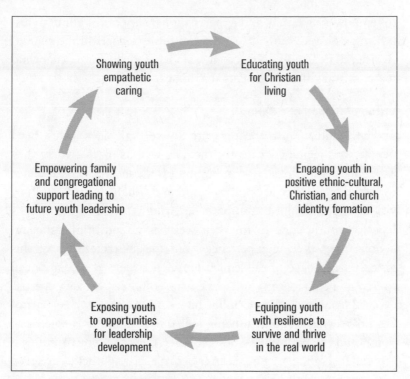

Figure 1.1. Visions of youth ministry.

ing the potential of all that is around us. Dreams don't happen in a vacuum. They are born in the real world, in a real situation.[6]

The vision statements of youth ministry leaders reflect both instances of visions emerging out of the call and visions that became modified or changed along the ministry journey. Their vision statements give us some handles on preferred focal points of ministry with black youth. Leaders were asked to respond to the question "What is your vision for youth ministry?" They revealed six specific themes. Their statements centered on (1) showing empathetic caring; (2) educating youth for Christian living; (3) engaging youth in positive ethnic-cultural, Christian, and church identity formation; (4) equipping youth with resilience to survive and thrive in the real world; (5) exposing youth to opportunities for leadership development; and

(6) empowering family and congregational support of youth ministry (to empower youth as present and future leaders in the church) (see fig. 1.1). Think about your vision based on the background material and vision statements that appear below.

Vision of Empathetic Caring

Today's youth ministry leaders are aware that black youth need people who genuinely care for them as well as places where they experience empathetic, unconditional love, concern, and guidance to help them negotiate both the good and tough stuff of life. As a vision for youth ministry, empathetic caring is fueled by the leader's love for youth, concern for their well-being, and nonjudgmental actions toward their experiences. But the characteristics of this vision extend beyond the leader. Earlier we learned of Amy's call to "come to Nineveh!" She came as a volunteer whose expertise evolved from her role as a public high school counselor. As part of her call story, she spoke of being pulled to respond to the needs of youth and the caring they deserve. Her vision statement built on this call by highlighting not simply her role as empathetic caregiver, but the congregation as the locus of empathetic caring.

> Amy's vision statement: "Youth ministry is all about making a place of belonging for youth, a comfort zone where they can tell their stories, ask their questions, be heard, and receive honest love, care, and guidance. It is about assuring that youth feel like the church is their church, God is their God, and the pastor is their pastor. It is not just their parents' or other adults' church. Rather, the youth can say, 'This is my church.'"

Amy reminds us of an empathetic caring community and a God who must become known by youth through our leadership and the church. Simply put, if we are going to be effective youth leaders, youth must see God in us. Amy gives us an important vision of an empathetic, caring leader and communal environment that youth must come to know and that leads to their experience of belonging. Moreover, she presents to us a vision for youth ministry that necessarily encompasses our own and our community's love growing out of God's love ("Every good and perfect gift is from above" [James 1:17]).

Vision of Educating Youth for Christian Living

Questions continue to arise in the black church about how to guide our youth in faithfully living the Christian life amid prevailing hopelessness, violence, and injustice. These questions come in the context of increasingly competitive, materialistic, and individualistic values in larger society that are influencing black life. The reality is that many of our youth are embracing values resulting in behaviors that undermine Christian living. And many of them don't realize that they have adopted an unreal and unrealizable hope. More and more of our young people want to pattern their lives after millionaire athletes and popular entertainers, fantasize about living like these heroes, and shape their views of life from media personages and music lyrics. For far too many, daily living is shaped by self-hatred or destructive life habits designed to meet their fantasies.[7] In addition, youth make social connections in our tech-saturated world that bring them closer to peers, out of sight to parents, and out of step with churches that are not tech-savvy. Some say the impact of technology is seen in "youth under the influence of tech-sparkle" to the degree that traditional church is foreign to them or has little appeal. When and if they attend church, they simply go through the motions of church liturgy.[8]

Of course, we can surely name youth who unapologetically identify themselves as Christians, are involved in church life, and, in addition, have a positive sense of their ethnic-cultural self, constructive life goals, and confidence in accomplishment. However, we face a profound challenge in how best to contribute to these youths' ongoing Christian walk as well as make this walk appealing to increasing numbers of youth for whom it appears to have little or no appeal. In the face of this challenge, leaders say that we have no choice! They are quick to say that the very lives of our youth are at stake; and to be blunt, the future of the church is at stake!

Leaders are sharing straightforwardly their vision of educating our youth for Christian living. Youth leaders tell of "keeping it real," knowing that this approach is the only way to effectively meet the needs of black youth and counter negative influences on their impressionable minds and hearts. In their sharing, they prompt us not simply to consider carefully but to embrace forthrightly a vision for youth ministry that centers on Christian living. What does this vision look like?

Recall Bernard's earlier story of being summoned by God to ministry at seventeen years old, and of making youth ministry central because of his recognition of our youths' need for Christian formation. He went on to state his vision.

> Bernard's vision statement: "Youth ministry has to be concerned with having Christ formed in the youth and making possible their realization that they have essential worth, dignity, and sacredness. Christian formation is needed so that our youth can begin to feel the pull of the hand of God on their lives, and [can] begin to have a sense of being called or drawn to what God is trying to do in their lives and in the world; and this means being led to give their lives meaning and purpose and direction in Christian vocation."

Bernard continued by saying that a space needs to be created for youth to seek a relationship with God, find their own voice, and cultivate their walk with God. He connected his vision to his call by saying, "So, in short, I have thought that in my ministry, I needed to respond to God's call on my life to work with youth in order to enable Christian formation to happen."

A number of other leaders also shared a vision that centered on Christian living. However, typically, their vision statements were couched in the language of Christian discipleship, as shown in Dana's image of youth ministry.

> Dana's vision statement: "Discipleship-focused youth ministry takes seriously youths' exploring and understanding the Word, really knowing what it means to live after the model of Jesus Christ and actually living it whenever they are inside the church walls, in the schools, at basketball games, or when they are walking down the block. It's living as Christians unapologetically everyday."

Vision of Forming Positive Ethnic-Cultural, Christian, and Church Identity

The importance of an ethnic-cultural emphasis as part of youth ministry with black youth cannot be overstated, because these efforts contribute to ethnic pride and the embrace of an unashamed black identity.[9] Yet we know from the Vision Quest research that where black history endeavors and Kwanzaa programs exist, they are often offered by organizations outside the church. Moreover, there is not always an exuberant affirmation of uses of Afrocentric material in youth activities.[10] Leaders' recognition that more is needed to connect our youth with their roots for the sake of their firm embrace of their African heritage and identity informed their vision statements. However, this focus in vision statements did not stand alone. The leaders' heightened consciousness that youth know little of the roots and history of the Christian church and of the denominational affiliation of the churches they attend prompted not simply vision statements centered on these dimensions, but actual uses of cultural materials such as Marvin McMickle's *Profiles in Black: Phat Facts for Teens*.[11]

Earlier we were introduced to Barry, whose call was prophesied before he was born. He carefully retraced the history behind his call to youth ministry leadership. It is not surprising that when asked about his vision for youth ministry, he continued with an emphasis on historical grounding.

> Barry's vision statement: "Ministry with black youth is about connecting them with our rich African and African American, Christian, and denominational histories and traditions that have promise for their affirming who and Whose they are and enriching the lives they live."

Vision of Equipping Youth with Surviving and Thriving Resilience

Our youth are no strangers to difficult life issues. They experience a full gamut of personal challenges, trauma, abuse, neglect, and pain. The impact of these realities is seen in self-esteem challenges, depression, grief, and anger that surface in their denigration of their physical appearance, lack of confidence, violence, and other negative behaviors. Their situations and behaviors cry out for coping skills, resilience, and healing. In light of the circumstances of far too many youth, it may be said that black youth are endangered. Much goes on that recruits them into suspect lifestyles and behaviors and the existence of relational refugees as shown in the burgeoning numbers of our youth who are incarcerated or otherwise in the criminal justice system.[12]

The earlier presented call of Anna revealed her experience of assuming that she was called to youth ministry simply because no one else was around to do it. The rest of her story was about what she described as the unimaginable situations of the youth she served. She told of struggling with what to do to make a difference and of feeling as though she failed in so many instances. But she spoke of being determined not to give up and of seeing small victories along the way. The fact that she found herself "staying the course" caused her to repeat her declaration, "I guess I'm called." She went on to share her vision.

> Anna's vision statement: "My vision is for youth ministry wherever it happens to hear the urgent plea of our youth for help, for change, for constructive action, and for justice. It is also for our ministry to leave no stone unturned in finding concrete ways to help our youth rise above the situations in which they find themselves by standing with them and equipping them with all they need to cope with the negatives of life."

Vision of Preparing Youth for Leadership in Today's Church and World

Some say that youth are the leaders of tomorrow's church and world, while others assert that they are *today's* leaders. In congregations where the latter view is true, youth ministry flourishes and congregational vitality thrives. This situation validates the notion that youth can and need to find and own their own skills for leadership from the pulpit to the wider life of the church to service in the community for their sake and for the sake of the whole community.

Angela's call story presented earlier also demonstrated the influence of leadership during the teen years on her continuing role as leader and call to youth ministry leadership after seminary. She told of being "at home" in the leadership role. Her personal story informed her vision statement.

> Angela's vision statement: "Any worthwhile vision must include giving youth a sense that there is a place and a purpose for them in the church and in life. That includes having them develop and participate in leadership. This vision extends to youths' claiming the role of servant leader based on the model of the servanthood of Jesus."

Vision of Empowering Family and Congregational Support

All of the youth ministry leaders in the Vision Quest study shared the central view that parental involvement in youth ministry is essential to its success. Yet they also unanimously agreed that it is not always possible to get parental participation. The reasons are many. We live in an era of unprecedented demands on heads of households, from two-parent families to single-parent and blended families, and from grandparents raising grandchildren to other kin providing primary care for children. Regardless of family configuration, stories abound of overwhelming responsibility to meet family needs, often amid limited or shrinking resources. Difficulties arise in negotiating busy schedules. Coping with a range of other family challenges requires time and energy.

Although there *are* parents like Deanna who get involved out of a vested interest in her children and others' growth and continued congregational participation, other parents are simply not available. A compounding problem occurs when congregational resources are limited or missing. Out of her enthusiasm for participation as well as her desire for more parental connection and commitment, Deanna stated her vision.

> Deanna's vision statement: "My vision is that parents and parental figures will see and claim their indispensable role in supporting ministry on behalf of our youth to the end that they—we—build up our youth and the whole Christian community in every way possible."

The Holistic Ideal

In his call story, Jeff indicated that he knew youth ministry was where God placed him prior to taking a senior pastor position. He further told of his interest in both youth and adults that leads him toward pastoral ministry with the hope of staying connected to youth ministry. He shared a key learning from observing youth and adults that applies to his ministry with youth. He called it "the holistic ideal," which he unpacked in a vision statement.

Jeff's vision statement: "Ultimately, a vision of youth ministry—like ministry for all ages—must be holistic. Ministry must encourage and shape lives by addressing persons' spiritual, social, educational, cultural, political, and financial needs. It tends to their spiritual formation (biblical literacy, Christ-centered learning, and Christian lifestyle expression). It looks after relational skills building and vocational direction. It highlights educational accomplishment that assures tools for ongoing living. It emphasizes ethnic-cultural identity, awareness, pride, and historical grounding. It creates ways of confronting justice issues and building economic sufficiency."

✓ CHECK IT OUT

Return to your reflection on your call story. Then recall that a vision for youth ministry does the following things:

- Paints a picture of youth ministry

- Develops at the intersection of our call and awareness of the needs and desires of youth

- Takes shape as we discern God's intention for our ministry with youth

- Appears as a ministry aspiration or target to reach

- Serves as an anchor for building youth ministry

- Connects with the church's vision or functions as a stimulus for congregational response

- Allows for revision

Consider the following:

- What vision do you have of youth ministry leadership? In what way(s) did it develop either from your call or your awareness of youths' needs or desires?

- What needs or concerns over your time as youth ministry leader signal your need to change or update your original vision?

- In what ways does your vision connect with your church's vision or invite congregational response?

NOTES

1. Ray's comment references 1 Corinthians 3:7.

2. This view is consistent with Janice C. Catron's in *God's Vision, Our Calling* (Louisville: Geneva, 2003), 1, that the way of Christians is "seeking God's direction, being open to God's voice, and following God's will. Accordingly, one of the great questions for Christians throughout the ages has been, 'What does God want of me and of the church?'"

3. See Carol Howard Merritt, *Reframing Hope: Vital Ministry in a New Generation* (Herndon, VA: Alban Institute, 2010), 6–7. While Merritt does not write from the standpoint of youth ministry, she makes a valid point that applies: monumental shifts are taking place in Christianity in general that call for reframing. Reframing allows for the recognition of new possibilities or seeing a situation from a different perspective. It also builds on the view that a great deal of hope is waiting to be kindled in the next generation.

4. See Edward P. Wimberly, *Recalling Our Own Stories: Spiritual Renewal for Religious Caregivers* (San Francisco: Jossey-Bass, 1997), 1.

5. The "four C's of keeping on keeping on" differ from and may be appended by the authors who entered the first names of Kurt and Josh, "3 Reminders from Your Youth Ministry Calling" indicate the following: (1) your calling keeps you humble, (2) your calling keeps you focused, and (3) your calling keeps you going. See http://www.youthministry.com/articles/leadership/3-reminders-from-your-youth-ministry-calling, found on www.youthministry.com, accessed June 22, 2012.

6. See George Barna, *The Power of Vision: Discover and Apply God's Plan for Your Life and Ministry*, 3rd ed. (Ventura, CA: Regal, 2009), 29.

7. See Anne E. Streaty Wimberly, "A Black Christian Pedagogy of Hope: Religious Education in Black Perspective," 155–78, in James Michael Lee, ed., *Forging a Better Religious Education in the Third Millennium* (Birmingham, AL: Religious Education Press, 2000), 157.

8. This view builds on findings in a national study of youth and religion reported in Kenda Creasy Dean, *Almost Christian: What the Faith of Our Teenagers Is Telling the American Church* (New York: Oxford Univ. Press, 2010).

9. Affirmation of the importance of an Afrocentric emphasis is set forth by Kenneth Hill, *Religious Education in the African American Tradition: A Comprehensive Introduction* (St. Louis, MO: Chalice, 2007), 132, who asserts that "the Afrocentric educator's task is to help Blacks rediscover their identity through a dialogue of African heritage, culture, and contemporary experience. . . . [A] person reaches self-awareness through remembering historical and foundational experiences."

10. The Vision Quest study found that 82.8 percent of the churches in the study offer Kwanzaa and/or black history programs. Yet 52 percent of such programs are offered by organizations outside the church. About 50.7 percent of respondents think it is most important for youth leaders to respond to issues specific to black youth. Yet only 37.3 percent think that it is most important to incorporate Afrocentric material during youth activities. Furthermore, 7.5 percent believe it is of the least importance that Afrocentric material is used in youth programs. Lastly, about 53.7 percent of respondents believe it is most important for youth leaders to be attentive to black history. The findings illustrate that a distinction is often made by respondents between black history and Afrocentric materials where the former resources may be more readily embraced and incorporated than the latter. These findings appear in Sandra L. Barnes, "Vision Quest 2009 Survey of Black Church Youth Leaders and Youth Ministry," unpublished document, December 2010.

11. Marvin A. McMickle, *Profiles in Black: Phat Facts for Teens* (Valley Forge: Judson, 2008).

12. See the complete exploration of meanings of "relational refugee" in Edward P. Wimberly, *Relational Refugees: Alienation and Re-Incorporation in African American Churches and Communities* (Nashville: Abingdon, 2000). Also see how the meaning of relational refugee is concretely shown and addressed in: W. Wilson Goode Sr., Charles E. Lewis, Jr., and Harold Dean Trulear, *Ministry with Prisoners: The Way Forward* (Valley Forge: Judson, 2011).

2

LEADING WITH HOPE

Up Close and Personal

*We know that all things work together for good for those
who love God, who are called according to his purpose.*
—Romans 8:28

Conversations with youth ministry leaders are often powerful moments of truth telling. During one of those times of conversation about what it's like to be a leader and what it takes to get and keep things moving in the best possible way, Shauna said with a sense of urgency, "Carrying out my role in this ministry is an awesome thing! I'm called to it. I love the youth. I'd also like to think I have some skills to do what is needed. What do I mean by that? I'd say first of all, doing what I do takes a heap of knowing myself—how I see myself, what I'm capable of, what I need to hold on to or to let go. For example, I wear lots of hats. At any given point in time, I'm a program director, mentor, coach, counselor, surrogate parent, teacher, fund-raiser, and cheerleader . . . all rolled into one. Am I capable of doing all of it? Well, it isn't easy to do everything that needs to get done! I do the best I can. At times I just have to stop and say to somebody, 'You do this or that!'

"There's something else. The hats I put on depend on the youth—my knowing *them*—where they are, where they come from, the stuff they face every day, and what and how they need to push forward in life with a sure faith. My kids are from the inner city. I hear their stories and know that times are tough and their needs are great. I owe it to them to take their situations seriously. I hope I'm doing okay. But truth be known, I wouldn't get very far if I didn't have trust and hope in God's being with me every step of the way! This ministry takes energy that's sometimes in short demand! It takes patience that's sometimes absent. I just have to cry out sometimes, 'Help me, Holy Ghost!' A lot of other things are needed too. But I'll stop by saying, Love for my youth carries me on. Plus, for sure, I have to be connected to God. Leaning on God gives me what I call holy boldness and commitment to do my best to make certain the best ministry for the youth! Yes, that's it: love, a big skill set, trust in God, commitment, and holy boldness!"

Striving for Excellence, Making Hope Come Alive

"What does it take to lead?" is a big question for leaders preparing for and entering youth ministry leadership. Shauna let us know that leading isn't always easy. Her story, along with so many others in the Vision Quest project is actually in line with the claim of Ronald A. Heifetz, a prominent leadership expert who says leadership comes without easy answers. In fact, he says, sometimes leaders may have no more than a question.[1] But hope-centered youth ministry leadership has a skill set with qualities, as Shauna said, that make possible a holy boldness even when answers are delayed or absent (refer to chart 0.2 on page 5 for a list of qualities and actions of leaders). If we have a vision and hope for our young people not simply surviving but thriving, we have to use excellence in making it happen.

What we bring of ourselves into the leadership role matters in the quest for excellent, hope-centered youth ministry. So does our knowledge of the youth we lead. And, as Shauna reminded us, we need spiritual resources to keep on keeping on! This chapter is about who we are as leaders, who the youth are in the ministry we lead, and what God has to do with our leadership. In what follows, join the conversation and check out where you are in your leadership journey.

Who Are We?

Youth ministry leaders are busy people. We often find ourselves too busy to look at ourselves and may, in fact, lose touch with who and Whose we are. At the same time, a key point made by leaders in the Vision Quest project was that carrying out hope-centered, excellent youth ministry leadership requires our ability and willingness to get in touch with ourselves as we enter this ministry and at various junctures along the way. An Ashanti proverb that is relevant to youth ministry leadership says, "If you understand the beginning well, then the end will not trouble you." Leaders are at the front end of youth ministry, and how things turn out depends largely on how we understand ourselves and what we do as leaders.

Shauna was not the only leader to highlight that leaders don't come empty into youth ministry. We bring qualities of the self—a skill set—into what we do and how we carry it out. These qualities have been shaped by our life experiences and varied kinds of preparation for the leadership role. However, in ministry, we don't stay the same, because ministry shapes us too. We develop new qualities and improve on the old. Considering youth ministry leadership, beginning it, and moving on in it offer us opportunities to get to know ourselves better and what we do best, need to throw out, and must improve. Taking this opportunity opens the way for us to affirm the beauty and power of self and discover or rediscover something of ourselves we did not know or had forgotten. It allows us to find places of challenge and the need to find an answer to a question about self. How may we get in touch with self? It happens by taking stock of and coming to grips with our motivations, our personal attributes, and the feelings we have about our ministry.

Motivation is what fuels our leadership and keeps us going. Chapter 1 told us that our calling and our vision are the sparks of a youth ministry leader's motivation. The call makes us say, "I have to do it!" And the vision says, "The ministry needs to be headed in this direction!"

Personal qualities are at the center of who we are as persons and leaders. In one sense, we may call them gifts that make up our personhood. But when embraced, they signal deeply held core values that we act on. They don't exist in a vacuum. We don't place them on a shelf. They are qualities that take on life through concrete behaviors and practices in the midst of our youth ministry leadership.[2] We choose to act on these qualities and build them up, especially ones that contribute to effectiveness in leadership and excellence in ministry. Looking closely at them prompts questions such as: Which actions have I taken or not taken? Why? Which actions are most needed? Where or with whom? What needs attention?

Leaders who took part in the Vision Quest project said that it is easy to take personal qualities for granted. We know we're supposed to have them and put them in practice, but we don't always pay attention to them. We take excellence and hope seriously when we do. Youth and leaders summarized the most important qualities of leaders in terms of love of youth, revering God's Word, and living God's way. They also added nine personal qualities considered as leadership musts. They are described below and shown in figure 2.1. Leaders must be:

Genuine. Being real with young people is critical! Youth respect their leaders when they see that they are authentic Christians, that they "walk the walk and talk the talk." Genuineness connects with respect and sincerity. In practice, leaders are able to raise concerns, invite discussion, give skillful feedback, and manage anger. We stand up for and live by the values we hold. We thwart it when we do not challenge negative attitudes and behaviors of youth or others connected to youth ministry. In the absence of genuineness, youth are quick to label their leaders hypocrites. Genuineness matters! (See Romans 12:9-10.)

Trustworthy. The quality of trustworthiness extends the understanding and expression of genuineness. It becomes active when leaders are consistently open, honest, reliable, and fair. The youth in our study said, "You can't say you're going to do one thing and then do something else, or play favorites. That's not right! Say what you mean and mean what you say!" Youth and leaders went further by describing trust building as being clear and fair about the expectations and the ground rules we leaders set for youth and for ourselves. In practice, trust building is being free and open to gathering, using, and sharing ideas of youth. Youth said trust wanes when leaders fail to follow through on plans, are not truthful or are only partially so, and are unpredictable. (See Ephesians 4:10-15.)

Accepting. Leaders who are accepting see youth as they are and are careful not to force a youth into becoming someone they aren't meant to be based on what the leader sees as real or right. At the same time, both leaders and youth said that sometimes youth do need to be shown more appropriate ways to behave. But a careful, caring way of addressing this need has to take place. Without initial acceptance and genuine caring before pushing for change, we risk being manipulative and even overbearing. We won't get anywhere. But when acceptance is followed by a caring way of addressing a need, the result can be a remarkable experience of reciprocity.

Consider the case of a youth who was chosen to be liturgist during Sunday morning worship. When the discussion was raised about dress code, she was adamant that her jeans and bright, multi-tinted hair should be accepted. The youth was invited by the leader to put herself in the place of the oldest church member who had been a champion of the youth ministry, and to imagine the attire this member might expect and why. After the role play, the youth said, "You know what? I see her point. What about if I compromise and keep my hair but throw out the jeans?" The leader agreed. When thanks were given to her at the end of the service, the congregation clapped—including the oldest church member. (See Romans 12:10; Philippians 2:3-5.)

Empathetic. With empathy, leaders understand the youths' and others' points of view. The empathetic leader understands what is being said and is "tuned into" others' emotions. We are able to step into a youth's shoes and be open to learning from her or him. We can be ourselves. We don't have to hide our real feelings, but we are able to imagine what it is like for the other person. In fact, when we are ourselves, we can allow the youth or others to be themselves.

A leader told the story of one of the young men in the youth group who seemed distraught. When the leader drew him aside and asked what was going on, the youth broke down and cried. He had learned of his mother's terminal illness and was dealing with the possibility of her death. Empathy on the part of the leader meant stopping to be present with the youth, encouraging him to share his feelings, asking the youth if there was something he would like the leader to do, and offering to be available for further times of sharing. (See Romans 12:15; Colossians 3:12-17.)

Optimistic. For many of the leaders in the Vision Quest study, optimism lay at the heart of faithful hope. In fact, one leader gave a staunch reminder that "faith is the assurance of things hoped for, the conviction of things not seen" (Hebrews 11:1) and followed the reminder with a caution that leaders won't get very far without this kind of optimism. Leaders also connected optimism with patience. Their position was that, even though we don't see results right away, we must be seed planters anyway. Or, as one leader said, "We must be patient and trust by faith that, if we plant, somebody will water and God will give the increase [see 1 Corinthians 3:5-9]. Yes, we would love to always see immediate results, but leading by faith, we accept that we don't have to. We trust that if we do all we are able to do, our kids will say, 'I really got what you said!'"

Courageous. One youth ministry leader called for the need to be "dangerously courageous." This leader meant that being courageous is sometimes risky. Other leaders agree and add that courage must be shown in a number of ways. Courage is a willingness to risk pushing for whatever assures a place for the youth in the life of the congregation—and for the budget to match. It's about pressing for and providing the means for youth to grow, to reach beyond the limits or blockages that sometimes paralyze black youth. Leaders have to be courageous enough to wear the multiple hats that Shauna talked about. According to the leaders, you also have to have courage sufficient to be the disciplinarian in the room without fear of losing popularity with youth. Sometimes, courage takes you outside your comfort zone into the roles of a coach who guides and encourages youth, a mentor who listens to the unimaginable story, and a surrogate parent who is needed in the throes of a youth's family crisis.

From the leaders' perspective, being dangerously courageous builds on optimism. It extends to "seeing what's possible in seemingly impossible circumstances and doing something about it. The reality is that, in more instances than we would like to name, our kids are endangered. They are walking past pockets of gangs. Some are recruited to gangs. Some are accosted by bullies. They walk into situations where a street gets locked down and they can't pass to get home or to church. Dangerous courage means that I do what I can and find a way to empower my youth so that they are able to cope with all of this, rise above it or manage it, and not get sucked into making dead-end decisions. My acting courageously is to pass courage on to my youth. It is being daring enough to struggle with them and not sacrifice the spiritual dimension. This means youth ministry that goes beyond fun and games assures their firsthand experience with Jesus Christ and opens the way for this experience to empower them to influence culture rather than be driven by it."

"In the final analysis," said another, "courage and commitment are twins. You have to have staying power!" (See 2 Corinthians 3:12.)

Creative. Even though leaders do not necessarily flaunt their gift of creativity, leaders have to be creative; and the mark of the creative thinker is being able to think outside the box. Creativity also means having the imagination to lead in a way that reaches young people where they are and takes them where they need to be. One leader described the way creativity gets played out: "I'm always amazed when working with young people, because you never know what you're going to hear or how they're going to respond. You pray that the real teacher in you shows up when you come together with youth. But the truth is that what we do is not—cannot be—etched in stone. We have to be flexible. We have to be creative. Yes, we need to come with an agenda, because young people can tell when we're not ready. So we have to be ready. But at the same time, we have to be sensitive to what's going on. We may need to decide that this is the day we have to do something else. Hopefully, God will give us discernment as to what that something else needs to be. Sometimes we just have to put the paper down and say,

'That's not what today's session is going to be about.' Surprisingly, sometimes these are our best times. We simply have to be creative and flexible and say, 'God have your way.'" (See Romans 12:6-8; 1 Peter 4:10-11.)

Humble. Leaders who are aware of who and Whose they are have a sense of their imperfections and are willing to admit that they make mistakes and are in need of ongoing learning and growth. Many of the leaders confessed, "I don't always get it right." Or, "I admit that there's a lot of trial and error in what happens." Or "on a scale of one to ten, with ten being the highest, I'm probably about a seven. There are some things I need to work on." One leader put it this way: "Being in this ministry has shown me where I'm weak and what I need to learn. This doesn't mean I lack confidence. I have confidence in my ability to care for, nurture, and minister to young people. It's just that I don't always have as much under-standing as I would like about what today's youth need. Honestly, it's up to me to learn what they need, and I try to do that. But it's not a once and for all thing. My own growth in serving them the best way I know how is to seek help figuring it out. One way I do that is to go to the youth and ask, 'How may I as pastor and our church best serve you? What do you need me and the church to do?' This tells them that I don't have all the answers and that some of the answers need to come from them. The youth are important teachers for me and my growth." (See Luke 14:11.)

Committed. Youth ministry leaders often don't stay long in their role. Most are volunteers who take on the leadership role for a limited period of time. Others are seminary students who serve as youth ministry leaders and then leave when they graduate. For some, youth ministry leadership is a stepping-stone to the position of pastor that is typically fulfilled in another location. When the youth ministry leader leaves, a new one is hard to find. When the leader leaves, youth grieve. Then they leave. Youth long for and need committed leaders who will hang in there with them as they move through adolescence. (See Galatians 5:22-23.)

Of course, there were other helpful qualities named by leaders and youth alike, such as being cooperative, determined, focused,

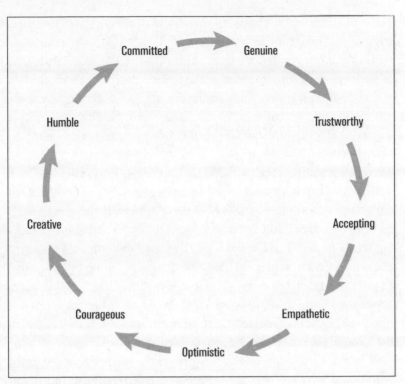

Figure 2.1. Personal qualities of leaders.

friendly, generous, punctual, resourceful, and responsible. But they made a special point of emphasizing the foregoing qualities. Leaders need to know that, whatever the quality, we may not get it right all of the time. We talked about youth leadership being like hip-hop dancing in the introduction, and when we turn on the music, hit the floor, and dance, we may find ourselves doing some improvising. That's not simply okay; it's necessary.

Feelings Matter in Leadership Effectiveness

Feelings or emotions have to do with what's going on inside leaders in the throes of ministry. Our feelings link with what we think about the ministry and our role in it and the actions we take to carry out that role. They are tip-offs to the value we or others assign to a program or activity, and they reveal our inner conflicts and interpersonal tensions. Emotions "tell it like we see and experience it." An example is the youth pastor who shared in a group of colleagues, "I'm feeling pretty good about where we are right now. Attendance is up. Parents are helping out. We've started a step group that's brought more young males from the neighborhood."

Another shared, "Hope? On a broad scale, I don't see it. On a small scale I do. In small arenas I see opportunities and potential for collaboration on projects. More is needed, but my thing is to keep moving forward!" Still another leader said, "I'm sitting here thinking that I'm just in a foreign land. I've tried everything I know to do, but I've never had a challenge like the one I'm up against now. I'm discouraged! I'm angry 'cause it just seems like nobody cares about the youth! You know what? If things don't improve, I'm out of there!" Others confessed there is no time to consider feelings in the fast-paced, jam-packed everyday tasks.

When we look carefully at our feelings, we become aware of where and why we find the greatest satisfaction, joy, and inspiration in youth ministry. We also admit to feelings of sadness, regret, and anger—and why we feel that way. We consider what or who "pushes our buttons" and what and who give us the most positive feelings. The point is that feelings cannot be ignored! For leaders to understand and respond to the feelings of youth and others with whom we relate in our ministry, we need to get in touch with our own feelings and find spaces to get them out. Leaders in the practice of ministry tell us that we place our health and ministry in jeopardy when we deny our feelings or fail to deal with them.[3] They can take us and our ministry to the next level or they can squelch a move forward. Help for facing our feelings may happen in several ways. Find a trusted confidant, mentor, or coach to be a sounding board. Form or join a youth ministry leaders group. Be sure to create times for spiritual self-care and recreation.

Knowing ourselves is all about staying in touch with our motivations, personal behaviors, and feelings. Doing so means that we look boldly at ourselves in the light of some important questions related to characteristics of the self in ministry leadership.

✓ CHECK IT OUT

Considering what you have read about motivations, personal behaviors, and feelings that are connected to youth ministry leadership, list what stood out the most. Which ones do you carry out the best? Which ones are the most challenging or need tweaking? Consider ways of tackling the challenges.

What Do We Know about Our Youth?

The question "What do we know about our youth?" is a loaded one because how we answer depends on what we're looking for and what we see. One way to know our youth is through our awareness of the developmental stage they are in. It means knowing about the areas that leaders in child and adolescent development name as physical, emotional, cognitive and educational preparedness, environmental, social learning, cultural, and spiritual (see chart 2.1). We may think we already know these things based on what we have already seen or experienced of the youth we lead or the ones who are in our families, but it's easy to lose sight of them or to overlook an area. It's worth reminding ourselves, especially because of those times when we find ourselves saying, "Did they just do that? Are you kidding me?" Take a look at the chart on the following page for a refresher.

But there are more than developmental factors to consider. In addition to features included in the chart, we minister to teens in their urban, suburban, small town, or rural locations. And we may abide by the claim that knowing our youth means acknowledging that they are part of the hip-hop generation and a peer group culture. We may be aware that many are in single-parent households or in blended families. Moreover, we may say that black youth

Chart 2.1. Adolescent Development[4]

Developmental Area	Developmental Focus
Physical	Youth are dealing with rapid physical and sexual development: growth spurt in girls 11–14 years; in boys 13–17 years. Puberty for girls 11–14 years with some younger than 11; boys 12–15 years.
Emotional	Youth are in the process of identity formation and experiencing sexual excitement and anxiety about their physical appearance and body image. May overreact to parental and other adult criticism, oppose adult standards, and rely on peer group for support. Toward middle adolescence (ages 15–17), youth examine others' values and beliefs and may become more positive about their self-image, but may struggle with racial identity, with being adopted or in a blended family, or with lesbian, bisexual, gay, or transgender identity.
Cognitive and Educational Preparedness	Youth begin to think logically and abstractly. They are able to consider a number of possibilities, plan a course of action, engage in self-analysis and reflection, draw insights, and problem-solve with ideas for multiple solutions. But cognitive development is also uneven and is impacted by emotions.
Environmental	Youth relate and respond to the environment they are in and grew up in. They are influenced by their family, peers, religion, schools, the media, community, and local to global events.
Social Learning	Youth see how others behave, choose behaviors to model, and voice criticism of behaviors they disagree with.
Cultural	Youth are aware of, have questions about, and want to know more about the culture in which they are born and grow up.
Spiritual	Youth raise questions about matters of life, faith, and meaning, and can make decisions about and commitments to a life of faith. They are open to prayer, have understandings about differences between hope and despair based on life experiences, and rely on others' models of faith living and others' help in sorting out and acting on their beliefs.

are known to face particular challenges, for example, as noted by stories of being profiled by police in department stores or elsewhere; by statistics of those who are incarcerated, are in gangs, or are perpetrating violence; and by numbers of those who are in jeopardy of leaving school or have dropped out, or are dealing with health issues, poverty, or early parenthood. But we also know youth who make the honor roll, graduate from high school and enter college, serve in church, lead in school and community organizations, and participate in community service. When we consider what it is we know about our teens, it is important that we take a close look at these realities and how we feel about them.[5]

Also consider that although youth in our ministry may fit in any one or more of the categories we've reviewed, each individual youth is *more* than the descriptions and *more* than what appears on a developmental chart. One size does not fit all! Black youth don't make up a homogeneous group. They vary in what and how they choose to live and express their identities.[6] The ones who come to youth meetings, Bible study, Sunday school, church worship, choir rehearsal, arts experiences, or community service and the ones who don't do these things have a story they live every day. The leader's task is to let youth know, "I see you. I want to know your story. I want to be a helper along the way and a guide who helps you link your story with God's story and what that means for your life." The truth is that youth today yearn to tell their stories in the face-to-face presence of a willing, caring listener in a way that contrasts with techno-connections where emotions are lost.

Tamiko told it like this: "I wasn't raised in church, but this girl invited me to her youth group. So, I agreed. I met the youth leader. She became like a mother to all of us. Because of her, I started going to church. She was the kind of person who would just listen to us. She would just listen; she didn't judge us. I don't talk a lot. I don't share my stuff with everybody. But I talked to her. I said she was like a mother. But she was also a friend. It made such a huge difference." The point here is that knowing youth includes being up on and learning from theory and descriptions about black teen life. But making excellent youth ministry come alive demands entering their stories, learning from them, and responding to them as God's agents and agents of hope. We will return to this later.

✓ CHECK IT OUT

Close your eyes, and picture the youth in your church—who they are and where they come from. Get in touch with their greatest needs. See in your

mind's eye the unchurched youth in the community around your church. Visualize their needs. Describe the church's outreach to them now or what needs to happen.

After building your mind's-eye portrait of the youth, create a written picture. Add anything that you missed when your eyes were closed. Include what you saw that surprised you, challenged you, or raised questions for which you will need to get answers. List some ways you will use to get to know the youth better.

It's a God Thing

Being an agent of hope is more than linking young people with God's story. A common point made by youth ministry leaders in the project was that, to be agents of hope, leaders themselves must be linked to God's story. In fact, their common agreement was that we must love God, love youth, and desire to show our love for both in our ministry with youth. They made clear that, in this thing called youth ministry leadership, we need to know ourselves as driven by a godly charge—our calling. We must be in touch with God and lean on God's for-us-ness in the nitty-gritty of all we do.

Recall Shauna's confession: "I wouldn't get very far if I didn't have trust and hope in God's being with me every step of the way! This ministry takes energy that's sometimes in short demand! It takes patience that's sometimes absent. I just have to cry out sometimes, 'Help me, Holy Ghost!'" Or another leader's statement: "I think we have to do what we do under the lens of our Christian walk and faith in Christ, because the issue that you can run into is that you get so far out there that you look back and you're wondering where Jesus went. We've got to keep our faith up front. And, we've got to hold on to hope in God, even though hope is sometimes a cliff-hanger, meaning you don't always know how things are going to turn out; but, with God, you're sure of the direction." Similarly, other leaders said that our knowing and claiming this kind of spiritual requirement is what motivates, nurtures, and guides our journey of leadership and makes our vision come alive. In fact, when faced with ministry challenges, leaders turned first to prayer before speaking with parents, youth, or pastoral staff.

Youth ministry leaders have a need for spiritual centering. This centering is pivotal to our seeing who we are and Whose we are, as well as perceiving our calling, our vision, and the particular capacities or behaviors we need for excellent hope-centered ministry. Through this centering, we claim hope and consecrate ourselves as representatives of God who are willing, as best we can, to "go the course" for the sake of nurturing youths' seeing God's presence and guidance in their lives. This knowing on the part of youth ministry leaders is akin to what Archbishop Desmond Tutu calls knowing "we are made for goodness by God, who is goodness itself."[7] And because we recognize it, we have exuberance—vim and vigor—in our ministry with youth. We have a necessary knowing of ourselves that propels us forward.

But how may we get in touch with ourselves and tap into the vitality of the spiritual dimension? Here are three key ways to do so:

- *Be quiet for moments of self-reflection.* We can become so busy and the demands on us can be so great that we lose the ability to own up to our need for quiet or the willpower to make it happen. Knowing our need for quiet time apart from the busyness of making youth ministry happen is critical for ongoing ministry vitality. We need quiet moments to ask, answer, and revisit the questions listed on page 57.

- *Be in conversation with God.* We have to be able to hear God's affirmation of our calling and assurance of our vision, and receive the guidance God gives us for youth ministry leadership. Some of us may have to exert extra effort to release ourselves from the tendency to become so busy that God cannot get a word in edgewise.[8] We need moments to be with God in a place where God can get through to us.

- *Be engaged in other spiritual disciplines.* Leaders can focus so much on what we need to do with and for our youth that we forget about own need to study the Word of God and allow Scripture to inform, guide, challenge, and inspire us in our personal walk. Reading the Bible, exploring meanings of

Chart 2.2. A Pull-It-Together Guide

Triumphs	Trials	The Way Forward
Motivation. Recall an event or experience that affirmed your youth ministry call and vision. How did the event or experience give you new or renewed motivation for your leadership?	**Motivation.** Tell about the biggest challenge to your motivation you have faced. What happened? How did it make you feel? What impact did it have on your leadership?	**Motivation.** How do you or may you build on the "wow" events or experiences so that you maintain high motivation? Create times to remember, recite, or write down your call to youth ministry and your vision for it.
Personal Qualities. What would you say are your best qualities? Remember a story of a time when you became aware that the qualities you showed in your leadership made a positive difference in the life of a youth or contributed to a positive ministry outcome.	**Personal Qualities.** Bring to mind an instance when you wished you had done something differently in your leadership. What did you do that brought about a difficulty or dilemma? How did you handle it? What have you learned from it?	**Personal Qualities.** In reading the chapter, what did you learn about your personal qualities? What new or renewed understandings of them do you have that may inform your present and future leadership roles?
Feelings. Get in touch with and share or write down what gives you the most satisfaction, joy, enthusiasm, or inspiration in youth ministry. Tell a story of an immensely satisfying experience. Pinpoint what made it so satisfying, and get in touch with the feelings that come as you remember it.	**Feelings.** Think of, share, or write down a time or experience when you felt a sense of sadness, regret, anger, or lack of control. What triggered your feeling(s)? Share any experience where something or someone has "pushed your buttons."	**Feelings.** Consider past moments of satisfaction, joy, enthusiasm, and inspiration you have experienced in youth ministry. Capture what happened that brought these feelings, and look for opportunities for these feelings to come again. When times arise that bring troublesome feelings, who would you name as a confidant, mentor, or coach to be a sounding board; or what youth ministry leaders' group might you join or start? What times for spiritual self care and recreation will you engage in?

Chart 2.2. A Pull-It-Together Guide (continued)

Triumphs	Trials	The Way Forward
Knowing and Learning from the Youth. Recount the names of your youth and their situations. Tell a story that captures who they are, their interests, and their needs. What short story would you tell about each one of them?	**Knowing and Learning from the Youth.** What would you say are the most challenging needs of your youth? Tell about any blocks you have met in addressing the challenges.	**Knowing and Learning from the Youth.** In reading this chapter, what did you learn about youth that affirms or reaffirms your understanding of who they are? What might you do differently now and in the future based on your understanding of the characteristics of adolescence?
It's a God Thing. Tell of a time when you felt empowered by God to accomplish a particular youth ministry program or task. Tell what happened and how your sense of empowerment came about. What spiritual discipline(s) have been most helpful to you in your role as youth ministry leader? In what ways have they been helpful?	**It's a God Thing.** Recall any instance or trauma in your leadership when you felt an intense need for God's presence and guidance. What happened? What did you do about it? Were you able to find a way through the situation or trauma? If so, how? If not, what are you doing about it?	**It's a God Thing.** How will you become aware of your need for spiritual centering? What spiritual resources will you call upon? Decide when, where, and how you will carry out the three keys to spiritual vitality mentioned in this chapter. Decide on additional ones that have meaning for you.

passages, and discerning ways they apply to our lives are important to our own growth. Worship that extends beyond our role of assuring worship experiences for youth, journaling, writing, and engaging in other creative artistic activities are other ways of enriching our spiritual lives.

✓CHECK IT OUT

Recall an experience in youth ministry when you were acutely aware of your need for God's presence and guidance. What happened? How did you call upon God? What response did you receive from God? What would you say about the nature of your faith as you go about ministry with youth? What opportunities do you create for self-reflection, prayer, and spiritual disciplines?

Pulling It All Together

Knowing ourselves, knowing our youth, and making use of spiritual resources are three musts in youth ministry leadership. Where you are now in all three of these areas may be where you need to be. If so, count this as a time of triumph. On the other hand, the "Check It Out" sections in this chapter may have called to mind some challenges you are facing. You are invited now to review alone or with a colleague or group the triumphs and challenges this chapter has called to mind. Review chart 2.2.

NOTES

1. Ronald A. Heifetz, *Leadership without Easy Answers* (Cambridge: Belknap, 1994), 2, 274–76, holds that when organizations look for leaders, they want "someone with answers, decision, strength, and a map of the future, someone who knows where we ought to be going—in short, someone who can make hard problems simple." He claims that leadership is shown by a willingness to face challenges, preserve a sense of purpose, take responsibility, and challenge others to help.

2. Ibid., 20, 271–73. Heifetz emphasizes that leadership is rightly understood as an *activity* rather than a set of personal characteristics. He further makes the point that leaders need to enter into self-examination and understand how they may function adaptively in situations.

3. See Gary L. Harbaugh, "Personhood of the Pastor, Significance of," in Rodney J. Hunter, ed., *Dictionary of Pastoral Care and Counseling* (Nashville: Abingdon, 1990), 910–11; William H. Willimon, *Clergy and Laity Burnout*, Creative Leadership Series, ed. Lyle Schaller (Nashville: Abingdon, 1989), 21–51.

4. The chart is adapted from material in charts appearing in Sedra Spano, Stages of Adolescent Development, http://www.actforyouth.net/documents/fACT%20Sheet05043.pdf; Stages of Development eCommons@Cornell.edu; and The Institute for Human Services for the Ohio Child Welfare Training Program, "Developmental Milestones Chart," October 2007, http://uppua.org, accessed September 28, 2012.

5. Lee H. Butler Jr., *Liberating Our Dignity, Saving Our Souls: A New Theory of African American Identity Formation* (St. Louis: Chalice, 2006), 61, 150. Butler makes the point that black youth exist with other blacks as part of the out-group at the hands of the prominent culture in-group. From this perspective, black youth are part of a distinctive cultural group. Therefore, when we consider what it is we know about them, it is important that we do it from an indigenous cultural perspective.

6. See Na'ilah Suad Nasir, *Racialized Identities: Race and Achievement among African American Youth* (Stanford, CA: Stanford Univ. Press, 2012), 4.

7. Desmond Tutu and Mpho Tutu, *Made for Goodness: And Why This Makes All the Difference* (London: Rider, 2010), 8.

8. The tendency of many youth ministry leaders to take on responsibilities that leave little time for self is akin to the challenging question posed by Gertrud Mueller Nelson, "Have we packed our lives with such a frantic pace in search of elusive happiness that God cannot get a word in edgewise?" See Gertrud Mueller Nelson, *To Dance with God: Ritual and Community Celebration* (Mahwah, NJ: Paulist, 1986), 19.

3
Growing as
Hope-Centered Leaders

*Let us run with perseverance the race that is set before us
looking to Jesus the pioneer and perfecter of our faith.*
—Hebrews 12:1-2

So much happens in the course of leading youth ministry. It's like running a race and getting steadily faster. But leaders can stay the course by remembering our call to it and our vision for it and by keeping an eye on hope and faith in our capacity to do ministry. Chapter 2 gave some additional steps for making youth ministry come alive. We considered key qualities we bring to youth ministry that show the heart of a leader. We considered characteristics that point to who our youth are. And we highlighted the spiritual center we must have to lead with hope. But there's more!

We bring what we know of ourselves, the youth we lead, and the depth of our faith into all we do to carry out youth ministry, including the "nuts and bolts" of leadership—specific kinds of know-how. We continue to grow in our understanding of this know-how as we get in touch with what to do and how to move youth ministry in excellent and hope-centered ways. This know-how involves skills and practices needed for leadership on the move that cause us, the youth we lead, and everyone else who sees the ministry to stand up and say, "Wow! That's great!" or "That ministry is onto something!" or simply "Hallelujah! Thank you,

Jesus!" In the Vision Quest project, leaders and youth alike told of two kinds of know-how: relational and operational. Let's consider each of these categories.

Relational Know-How

There's no mistaking the necessity of being able to relate to youth. "To put it bluntly," said one leader, "if you can't relate to these kids, you may as well give it [the ministry] up!" As we indicated in the introduction, relational know-how, also known as relational aptitude, pertains to personal effectiveness skills that leaders need to connect with youth, care for youth, collaborate with youth, and celebrate youth. Having these skills means that leaders know where youth are and have a plan for reaching them.

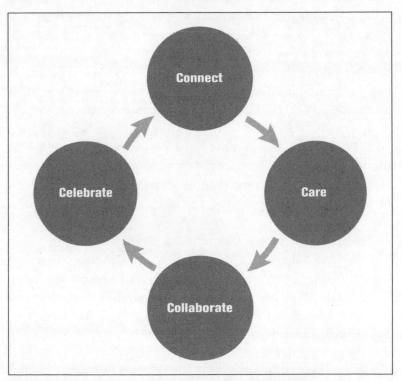

Figure 3.1. Relational capacities of a youth ministry leader.

Connect with Youth

Leaders get to know youth and discover what youth ministry can do to meet their needs when we connect with them where they are. Connecting refers to a leader's skill in making direct personal contact with youth. How can we do it? In telling a story of connection, Rev. T shared, "Throughout my ministry I have always valued knowing all of God's children and visiting with them in their homes. It was important to me because a pastor visited our home when I started going to church without my parents. That left me feeling that the church really cares and represents a God who cares for people. So, when Nancy, a teen, came to our church with three of her siblings, I felt compelled to visit them so I could know them better and get to know their family. Their mother, a single mother, was not coming to church with them."

Rev. T continued, "The main goal was to let the youth and her younger siblings know that they are important to God and they are important to me and the church. Because of my visits, Nancy and her siblings became more open and began participating in more activities at church. Nancy joined the choir. Her mother also started coming to church when she could. The family's openness increased to the point that all the children began sharing with me their progress in school that kept showing improvement in their grades. The visits proved to me that visiting youth regularly is the way I can connect more with them, understand them better, inspire them to do the best they can, and connect with their families."

Leaders' connection with youth is a nonnegotiable part of the leader's relational aptitude. Rev. T's example is one way. There are others. Youth ministry leaders get to know young people best when we see them in places where much of their daily life occurs—at home, at school, and in the neighborhood. Ideas for connecting include the following:

- Make home visits. These visits open the way for seeing a youth's everyday environment and for meeting parents or guardians and other family members.

- Attend school events like plays, concerts, sports events, and other competitions. Through these events, we support youth and discover their interests and gifts.

- Stop by neighborhood basketball courts, football practice fields, and other popular youth hangouts. At these spots, we see the friendships youth form and their ways of interacting with one another, and we come in contact with prospective youth ministry participants.

- Recognize special days in youths' lives, including birthdays and times when they receive awards, with calls, cards, or e-mail or text messages. Also recognize losses, such as the death of family members and friends.

Following are some other useful ides for connecting with youth: *Break the old code of connecting.* Connecting with today's youth requires leaders to take on a "techie" role. This means being aware of and willing to connect with youth using social media. Shelby, a teen in our study, said, "I don't do letters. Tweets are my thing." Youth minister Lee advised, "We absolutely miss the connection with our youth when we think they should rubber-stamp or go along with our ways of doing things. Many of us have to move beyond a mind-set based on the past. Our teens have a techno-code of connecting that's not going away. The world is changing! Truthfully, the teens' world has already changed!"

Brenda, a leader, told how she broke the code of connecting: "I knew I had to start getting in touch with my youth in the way that's familiar to them. So I began it all with texting. . . . I began sending out a weekly mass text message to everyone who had cell phones, and I'd get the cell number for anyone who was new or a visitor. In turn, I'd make sure they had mine. When I first did it, they were like, 'How do you know that?' And I'm like, 'I'm not really *that* old,' but okay, whatever. Now I've advanced to tweeting and using Facebook. The truth is it changed me! It changed the way the youth felt. They became more involved. It opened lines of communication apart from how we relate in the youth group! So sure, we leaders need to get real and be open to change."

A tip from another leader was to "get educated on youth culture in order to enhance connections. You don't have to speak their language, but it's good to know the current lingo, including texting codes. Find out what's showing on MTV and BET, the popular rap artists and their messages. But be ready to share your own 'picks' on TV and your music and why."

Break from church youth connections and include community youth connections. Althea, a leader, brought forth still another aspect of connection. She reminded us that "connecting with youth is not simply an in-church thing with in-church youth. There is a larger community out there with youth who need to be seen and reached. It just takes making the effort to get out and do it, even when it's unpopular to the folk in the congregation." In one case, the youth ministry leader canvassed the neighborhood for youth by going house-to-house and inviting unchurched youth to join a step group and in another instance, a drumming group. Other leaders "hung out" with youth at a local YMCA, neighborhood basketball courts, school bus stops, and introduced themselves to principals in order to make visits in high schools. One leader said, "It's a slow process, but if you keep at it, it pays off! Of course, you often have to work with the congregation to get them ready to receive new youth; and sometimes you have to stand in between these youth and members and 'holler' loudly, 'These are our kids! They belong to us! Welcome them!'" What is important is that real ministry includes these kinds of connections with youth and efforts to bridge the gap that too often exists between children of families who grow up in the church and children in families who are more recent neighborhood residents. Real connection erases the "us" and "them." When we make good on real connections and real ministry, we are living out the real gospel of Jesus Christ!

Break out of connections made only by leaders. One leader in our study had this powerful message: "Youth know how to reach other youth. The truth is, youth come because of other youth. So why not have youth make connections with youth? We don't have to do it alone." In one instance, two youth group representatives brought to the leader the suggestion that the group carry out a

"Walk the Walk, Talk the Talk" campaign in their neighborhood of many unchurched youth that also included their friends. The youth prepared flyers that said: WANTED! YOU! and that listed youth group activities along with the place and times of the meetings. Every Saturday over the period of a month, youth set out two by two (one male and one female), one pair in the morning and another in the afternoon. When they saw youth from the neighborhood at school or on the street, they made a special point to connect with them and invite them to "check us out" at the next youth group meeting. As the month ended, the group of ten teens had grown to sixteen. The youth saw this growth as a start and their job as getting and keeping everybody moving ahead together.

Real and hope-centered connections of leaders

- reach youth where they are
- reach youth in ways that are youth friendly and welcome youths' reaching back in their own way
- bridge the gap between churched and unchurched youth
- give youth opportunities to connect with other youth

Care for Youth

Making connections with youth is not an end in itself. It extends to real care leaders give to youth. One teen in our study remarked, "We need them to care, to be there at our lowest and highest points—be there when we're going through rough times." Both leaders and youth say that care depends on the leader's availability, responses to real-life stories of youth, and service as trusted mentors.

Be available. The availability of youth ministry leaders to youth is a two-way relational venture. Leaders connect with youth where they are and are present with them during youth group meetings or other activities. In addition, youth are able to reach the leader. Availability translates into leader-youth relational connectedness that has the Christian growth and development of youth at the center. One leader said, "I'm going to go and be with my kids when they need me. But they can also text me, Facebook me, follow me on Twitter, e-mail me, call me. I try to be a model of the Christian life the youth can pattern their lives after. I can't just fall off the face of the earth when one of them needs help. If I do that, how will they learn to care for one another and be concerned about the needs of others as they grow in the Christian life? So I have to be available! On another note, this may go beyond what somebody considers necessary boundaries. But there's another reality. If I'm not available, many of my kids are going to miss out on some answers—some information—they want and need for their lives right now."

The leader continued, "Are there limits to availability? Sure! A leader has to be very clear about setting and maintaining boundaries and being very careful and assertive about how the relationship works, which includes what the limits are. So it's cool to be open, accessible. I'm here. I tell them this. But I also say, 'Here's the way this has to go down. If it's after this time, you'll need to leave me a message, and I'll get back to you. There will also be some things you put on the table that I'll have to think about and get back to you on, and some things I might not have an answer for.' Being real and up front is key. They can handle it. That's part of building and keeping a strong relationship."

Boundaries to availability are also needed in other matters, particularly when the leader feels thrust into a parental role or into a youth's family situation. For example, as leaders, we may want to help youth walk through the rough "stuff" of life or baggage they are carrying from their family relationships related to divorce, blended families, cases of absent fathers, and abusive relationships, for example. But, we have to be honest with our gut feelings and self-assessment that a situation calls for more than we are capable of giving and, as a result, we need to seek help from or refer youth to counselors. Also, in cases when a parent is leading youth ministry and has teens in it or when the leader is not the parent, the leader may need to say to a youth, "I cannot tell you what to do. What I can do is help you sort out some options to draw on for coming up with the best solution. But it's your decision." Nonparent leaders also need the kind of relationship with youth to be able to say, "Your parent or guardian has the right to know about, give permission for, or join with me to carry out any activity that is under my leadership." And, as leaders, we have to be free to say clearly that in the case of threat of harm to a youth or others, "It is my duty to get needed help." There is a thing called the ethics of availability—certain principles or moral values that come into play in the matter of leader availability.

Get in touch with the needs of youth. Leadership on the move is fully engaged ministry that has the needs of youth at the center. We show care when we look, listen, and make ourselves available to act as best we can on the particular stories of black youth demanding attention. Whether in urban, suburban, small town, or rural areas, the stories youth live every day matter! Depending on our church location, youth in and beyond our churches may appear to "have it all together" or may act in surprising or even hard-to-handle ways out of anger, frustration, or hopelessness as the result of their day-to-day experiences. Hearing stories through home visits and other contacts makes us aware of youth's experiences, such as low self-esteem; pressure to succeed; trauma from family situations—for example, divorce, blended families, single-parent families, adoptive families, foster families, grandparent- and other kin-headed families, poverty, or homelessness; school failure or drop-out and school-related issues such as bullying; poor health and/or nutrition; teen parenthood; abuse; drugs; youth detention; lack of future goals; or a host of other crises and concerns.

This is tough stuff! What can leaders really do? Over and over again, leaders confess that simple how-to answers don't always work.[1] Yet the answers are clear. First, the know-how of caring leaders has to go beyond society's label of "at-risk youth" to the point of declaring that action can be taken for the youths' sake. Leaders must further declare within them and with whomever else will listen that without action we surely have a "village at risk" of losing valuable and powerfully needed leaders for today's and tomorrow's church and society.

Second, admit that a youth ministry leader cannot minister to teens alone. Appeals made to and support received from congregations can make a big difference. But when support is not fully present, resources from and partnerships with community agencies can become a critical line of defense. For example, leaders tell of helpful partnering with Boys and Girls Clubs and with already existing community health initiatives for youth in hospitals and clinics, drawing on community-based speakers to address identified topics. They also recommend maintaining a list of legally responsible parents'/guardians' names and contact numbers for needed consultation and assistance, as well as a list of web-accessed youth service hotlines for

- HIV/AIDS and sexually transmitted disease information
- alcohol and drug treatment and prevention
- mental health agencies
- eating disorders and obesity
- suicide threats and prevention
- rape counseling
- LBGT (lesbian, bisexual, gay, and transgendered) resources
- runaway youth

Be a trusted mentor. In this age of distant high-tech relationships, black youth still need up-close, trusted, caring one-on-one and group mentoring that allows them to tell their stories, raise questions, test out the answers, cry, laugh, and be consoled. Youth ministry leaders are in a special position to take on this significant caring role. The role as mentor also opens the way for leaders to become aware of youths' stories and specific needs for care. As mentor, the leader functions variously as a trusted guide, confessor, friend, teacher, and role model who creates an emotional bond and safe space where youth feel free to "tell it like it is." But for them to "tell it like it is," we must listen, listen, listen! One of the biggest criticisms youth have of ministry leaders is that we are so busy talking and telling them what to do and what not to do that they can't get a word in edgewise.

Leaders tell of experiencing what Dr. Ron Taffel calls youths' "conspiracy of silence," which has to do with fear of being judged and not ratting on peers for whatever reason.[2] However, leaders are very clear that when youth experience us as trusted, caring listeners who create time with them, invite them to share whatever is on their hearts, and withhold judging, the stories tumble out. After all, they are in search of and in need of healing.[3] Are there times when leaders see an apparent need for a youth's behavior or attitude correction? Sure! But youth must first feel deep in their heart that they are loved, welcomed, and belong! And only then is it possible to move into a conversation that invites youths' personal look at their behavior, their responsibility for it, and how to address it.

As youth ministry leaders, we take on the mentoring role as *Christian* mentors with the express purpose of creating a space for youth to explore the promise and challenges of the Christian life and what it means to accept responsibility for it. Mentors become a part of teens' life journeys and seek to point them to God's story. Leaders recognize the biblical precedent for this role in Jesus who, as mentor of the disciples, raised and answered deep questions about matters of faith, such as deliverance (Mark 9:28), eternal life (Luke 18:18-22), the importance of parables (Matthew 13:10-17, Mark 4:13-20), and signs of the end (Mark 13:4). We also see mentoring in the Old Testament stories of Jethro's mentorship of Moses (Exodus 18:1, 6-27), Moses' mentorship of Joshua (Deuteronomy 3:28), Elijah of Elisha (1 Kings 19:19-21; 2 Kings 2:9-14), Eli of Samuel (1 Samuel 3), as well as in New Testament examples of Elizabeth's mentorship of Mary (Luke 1:39-56) and Paul's mentorship of young Timothy (1 Timothy 1:1-11, 18-19 and 2 Timothy 1:1-12).[4]

How may leaders make mentoring come alive? As Christian mentors, invite youth into what may be called "holy conversations" that help youth connect their stories to God's story—and what this story means for everyday living.[5] Ask them to raise and answer questions in the first person such as: Who am I as a black teen? Who am I or who do I desire to be as a *Christian* black teen? Why am I here? Where am I going in life? What should I do in my life or my situation right now? What's God got to do with it? In mentoring taking place during youth group meetings, propose a topic for group discussion based on observations of the youth and issues they face. Help them move from problem to problem solving by framing questions such as: What will you do with this concern? How will you handle that issue? What might this suggest for your actions with others in the group and others outside the group? What has happened here that gives you some ideas for your vocational direction? In whatever way the youth share of themselves with us, we consider ourselves to be on holy ground, in need of the Holy Spirit's guidance ourselves.

As mentors, leaders may "speak forth" questions for youth to consider: "Have you given any thought to . . . ?" Ask youth in the group to make recommendations or give words or gestures of affirmation and support. At times youth need to hear: "You are a valuable creation of God. You are a valued and beautiful (or handsome) human being. You know what? You're loved by God, and I love you too." Draw on Bible passages such as Psalm 139:1-18 to provide biblical affirmation of a valued identity. As leaders, we may share our own stories of our teen years that enhance youths' identification and bonding with us.

It is important to note that the leaders' description of their mentoring role points to three main mentoring functions:

1. *A pastoral function* focused on giving care that helps youth tell and address stories of their everyday lives, who and Whose they are, and the direction of their lives.

2. *A prophetic function* that challenges the youth ministry leader to look at the nature of Christian life, the youths' commitment to it, and ways of living it in everyday life.

3. *An apostolic function* focused on the youth ministry leader and the leader's model of Christian life.[6]

The following chart describes these functions in terms of the youth ministry leader as pastor, prophet, and apostle.

Youth ministry leaders who take on the critical task of caring for black youth are in line with the traditional care given in black communities out of the need to sustain black life and affirm black identity in our ongoing experiences of racism. In giving this care,

Chart 3.1. Mentor Functions of the Youth Leader

The Youth Leader as Pastor	The mentoring leader as pastor focuses on creating a welcoming, safe space for youth to share their stories. As pastor, the youth leader is concerned about what is happening to youth in their everyday lives, their views of and feelings about life, how to address life's struggles, who and Whose they are, and God's purpose for their lives.
The Youth Leader as Prophet	The mentoring leader as prophet challenges youth to look intentionally and carefully at the Christian lifestyle, how they are living it now, and what is yet needed to live it in everyday life. As prophet, the mentor takes on the role of spiritual director who helps youth get in touch with their spiritual gifts and what it means to use these gifts for the good of others. In this role, the mentor helps youth look carefully at how Christian discipleship is lived at home, school, church, and in the community.
The Youth Leader as Apostle	The mentoring leader as apostle centers on the self's character and modeling a life of integrity. The mentor recognizes and assesses the self's responsibility for youth, the self's ethical or moral behavior, and the self's accountability to God as God's representative or as "God-bearer" and the example of Jesus Christ. The leader also takes the position that leaders make leaders and is about developing youth who will step into the leadership role.

leaders act on a very real knowing that care has been and continues to be needed to assure that black persons survive and thrive. This is still the case for black youth. In fact, if we take seriously the critical task of caring for our youth, it must be nothing short of what Shawn Ginwright describes as "enacting radical care" that points to intentional, essential and uncompromising care."[7]

Some points to remember. When connecting with and caring for youth, as leaders, we must do the following:

- Be available through various kinds of communication. But be clear about how and when youth can reach us and about when our time is private.

- Be available to respond to special circumstances in youths' daily lives. But be clear about what we can and cannot do. We must not make promises we can't keep.

- Be available as observers of danger signs. Know when and where to seek help and get it. Maintain a list of youth service hotlines that we may use with youth and/or in collaboration with parents and guardians.

• Keep parents informed and seek permission for activities and trips. Make clear to youth that we are not their parents or guardians.

• Be available as mentors who function as pastors, prophets, and apostles.

✓ CHECK IT OUT

How do you connect now or would you like to connect with youth in your congregation? In the community? Review activities you have used to care for youth. What do you do to welcome and hear their stories? In what ways would you say you function now or may yet function as pastor, prophet, and apostle? What difference have you seen or would hope to see in youth as the result of your pastoral, prophetic, and apostolic functions? What changes would you make about how you connect and care for the youth you lead?

Collaborate with Youth

Collaboration adds to leaders' connecting with and caring for youth in ways that promote two-way connections. As collaborators, leaders counter youths' accusation: "They don't listen!" One youth described collaboration this way: "Being there for us is not just to tell us what we need to do, but also to ask us what's going on and what we think, what we need to improve on, and what needs to be done. If they're for us, then they're with us and get involved with us by hearing what we have to say." The "Walk the Walk, Talk the Talk" campaign is an example of a leader's not simply hearing but responding to what was heard. In other cases, collaboration resulted from a leader's hearing the message of teens about worship that is too traditional or meetings and activities that leaders planned *for* them.

In one instance, the leader said, "I got the message loud and clear! We've done several things with regard to worship. One was developing a youth-led service every fifth Sunday. Another was making sure some sort of youth leadership is part of every worship service. We've had processionals with music chosen by them and youth holding banners made by them, youth as liturgists, music by the youth choir, and an intergenerational liturgical dance group and praise team. There's more to do. But we're working on it." In other congregations, youth serve as Sunday morning speakers; youth accompany pastors' sermons with drama presentations, rap, and spoken word; and youth help to develop and guide a variety of high-tech approaches to worship (see chapter 6).

Collaboration involves listening to, hearing, and learning from youth. Without this attentiveness, leaders cannot know or be fully responsive to them. Moreover, in order to go beyond listening to hearing youth, leaders show the personal qualities mentioned in chapter 2 that are part of our personhood, such as genuineness, trustworthiness, acceptance, empathy, optimism, courage, and commitment.

✓ CHECK IT OUT

Consider what you've read about collaborating with youth. What story would you tell of your success in collaboration? What added or new kinds of collaboration come to mind?

Celebrating Youth

Brian said with great emotion, "Our youth need to know that they are important to us. They bring life and energy to us today. They are our future. In fact, there is no future without them. But do we let them know it? I'm convinced we don't do it enough. We need to show it!" Other leaders tell of seeing youths' eyes light up on Youth Day when a youth who has gotten no recognition elsewhere hears his name called, or when the special giftedness of a youth is revealed for the first time in her spoken word. The leaders' comments center on the celebration of youth, which is all about affirming and appreciating youth as a gift—God's gift[8]—

and showing delight in their presence, honor in their accomplishments, and hope for their future.

Making the point to celebrate black youth is critical in light of the tendency of mass media to broadcast negative images of our youth.[9] The responsibility of youth ministry in black churches to highlight the value, giftedness, and promise in youths' presence provides a powerful message that is needed to overtake the media's negative depiction of black teens. For celebration to happen, the youth ministry leader is key! Leadership means making celebration happen in youth group meetings and in wider congregational environments. How? Youth leaders shared with us some examples:

- A celebration can take place in every youth group meeting by telling all of the youth that they are loved and their presence is a blessing. Black youth need to hear this message over and over again.

- Celebration can happen in youth groups when birthdays are celebrated; when attention is given to academic, artistic, athletic, and other accomplishments; and when leadership is shown within the group, in church, and in outside activities such as community service.

- Celebration is warranted in youth group meetings when a youth has overcome an adversity that he or she has shared with the group. Overcoming failure, recovering from illness, and making it through a harrowing event are reasons to celebrate.

- Congregations celebrate when they schedule special times of recognition, such as Youth Days or Youth Sundays, galas, or banquets that honor high school seniors and others who are advancing in education.

- Special means of celebrating within congregations include a "Youth Hall of Fame" where a picture of every youth appears on a bulletin board and notes of birthdays and accomplishments appear in church newsletters and on church websites.

Celebrating black youth doesn't just affirm, honor, and express hope for them. Celebration communicates an open-armed welcome! We say more in chapter 5 about what it means to welcome youth, and we provide strategies for making it happen.

✓ CHECK IT OUT

What kinds of celebration of youth have taken place in your youth ministry?
How may celebration of youth in your youth group happen in new ways?
How may celebration of youth in your congregation happen in new ways?

Operational Know-How

Excellent and hope-centered youth ministry happens in large part because of leaders' relational know-how. Good relationships build good youth ministries. However, leaders need operational know-how, or operational aptitude, to carry out youth ministry programs and activities. In the operational part of leadership on the move, the leader functions as decision maker and teacher, administrator, and evaluator as shown in figure 3.2.

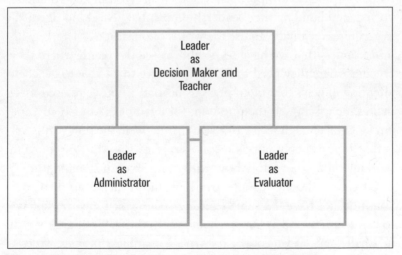

Figure 3.2. Operational functions of a youth ministry leader.

The Leader as Decision Maker and Teacher

Leaders need operational know-how, or operational aptitude, to decide on and carry out youth ministry purposes, programs, activities, and approaches that will best serve black youth in a particular church and community. Leaders in the Vision Quest project said again and again that one size does not fit all when it comes to making operational decisions. Ideas that work in one place may not work in another. So choosing what is best happens *on location* and in response to the youth in our congregation and those we seek to reach beyond the church. But there are some common areas of focus. One leader pointed out the ability to "plan relevant activities that meet the holistic needs of black youth wherever we are." A youth called it "the leader's ability to give us activities that help us get closer to God and ones that keep us out of the street and in the church." These common areas of focus expand to take into account characteristics of youth presented in chapter 2. We give detailed attention to programs and activities based on these characteristics in chapter 5.

Added to the ability to decide and plan is leaders' ability to carry out or teach what is planned. Teaching places on leaders' shoulders the responsibility for approaches that engage youth, keep them involved, and build up their leadership potential. This kind of teaching requires creativity. To use the words of one leader, "I agree with other leaders that we have to be able to see the youth where they are and where they need to be. But we have to be able to get their attention in ways that often press us beyond what we're used to. It makes me ask myself the question, for example, 'Am I ready and am I a good enough techie to reach them?' Well, the honest answer is that I'm probably not as techno-savvy as I need to be, but I'm working on it. That know-how with today's youth is mandatory!"

Of course, leaders cannot overlook the reality that all of our youth do not have the same learning style, which means we have to use a variety of ways to teach and reach them. We engage youth in small- and large-group experiences; readings; movies, videos, and PowerPoint presentations; simulation, drama, arts, and music activities; social media contacts and conversation; play; and other tools the youth suggest that capture their attention and get them invested in ways that contribute to their formation as black Christians who will go beyond surviving to thriving.

The Leader as Administrator

Excellent and hope-centered ministry depends on administrative tasks such as arranging times, places, and resources for youth ministry. But leaders in the Vision Quest project told again and again that having ideas about what to do and making them happen are often two different things. Leaders know that having a welcoming place to meet, relevant materials, and parental support, as well as material and financial resources, is paramount in assuring excellent youth ministry. Yet these things often constitute the most difficult challenges faced by leaders. It takes a courageous and creative administrator to work through and sometimes around obstacles to ministry success and excellence. For one thing, they say, the conflicts between the needs and the obstacles make certain that we "stay in our prayer closets."

But there are other practical ways to make things happen. One promising approach is simply to draw attention to the youth program by posting in the church and around as many places as possible in the community what the youth are going to do on a specific day, time, and place. Use the youth to publicize events, spread the news yourself to adults, and wait for people to "catch on".

One leader used this line of attack with a step group, using the leader's knowledge and experience of stepping. The leader told of the slow process and of the demand for patience. But what began with a few swelled as a few youth mastered steps punctuated with Christian rap. At one point, the leader felt the time had come for the few to "shine" in a Sunday worship service. Even though some eyebrows were raised at this new innovation in worship, a number of attendees wanted to know how other youth might get involved. A few more youth joined. Based on suggestions by the youth and a parent, and with the permission of the pastor and church committee, the leader scheduled a "Crunk for Christ Step Meet on the Street" in front of the church. Community residents came to see what was happening. More youth joined. Parents, grandparents, and other relatives came to see them when they presented in later church services. Then the group began to receive invitations to perform outside the church, and the youth ministry grew as a result.

In another example, a volunteer youth leader in a small town congregation connected with volunteer leaders in other churches and developed a cluster youth ministry. In still other cases, leaders met with parents, the pastoral staff, coworkers, and advisory committees to brainstorm and decide youth ministry directions, programs and activities.[10] In every case, the examples shared by leaders show that administration has a very real relational component to it. Typically, administration isn't the solitary task of the leader. Others are needed and must be sought to make ministry happen.

Some tasks, however, are the sole responsibility of the youth ministry leaders. Among these tasks is keeping good records, such as a youth roster, attendance records, and program and event records with anecdotal information about event details and outcomes. The reason for carrying out these kinds of administrative tasks is, said a leader, that "records are a way of leaving the footprints of our ministry for whomever steps up to the plate as we leave. Our successor deserves to have some knowledge about what happened so that she or he can regroup the youth ministry for the future." Other leaders in the project told of arriving at a congregation as a new youth ministry leader with a desire to know what had previously happened from the former leader's perspective. New leaders welcome this kind of information in order to determine how best to proceed.

The Leader as Evaluator

We noted in the introduction that many leaders in the national study did not have plans or measures to evaluate what they were doing in youth ministry. However, the continuation of hope-centered ministry depends on hearty critical reflection on every aspect of youth ministry. This is an essential part of our operational aptitude. In the words of one leader, "We ought to have a record of what we've done—to affirm what we've done, assess what we've done, and have a basis for changing what we've done to something different or better." In this way, record keeping becomes an evaluative tool that reveals the outcomes of youth ministry and what is needed to continue or discontinue. Evaluation happens because leaders take it seriously and because hope-centered ministry depends on hearty critical reflection on every aspect of youth ministry.

In reality, there are two kinds of evaluation: *formative* and *summative*. *Formative evaluation* is an ongoing means of measuring outcomes of what we undertake with youth. In formative evaluation, leaders create time during or after youth group meetings to ask youth, "How are we doing? What has this session or experience done for you or meant to you? How is the youth group helping you? What have we missed? What would you like to see us do?" Questionnaires, inventories, and short tests may be given to gauge what youth have gained from an experience, exercise, or meeting topic. Leaders may also keep a journal of personal observations or anecdotes of group and individual youth responses to track changes, improvement, or concerns needing attention.

Summative evaluation gives us a measure of what has happened to youth in our ministry over the long haul. Summative evaluation takes place at the end of a planned program or extended period of activities. It requires youth and leaders alike to recall what has taken place over a period of time, the impact it has had on them, and what might yet be done. Through this evaluation, we want to find out what has been accomplished in the form of specific outcomes for the entire group and for individuals as well as the extent to which set goals have been met. We may gather this information from youth in an open discussion or through written responses, inventories, or individual interviews. We may expand this kind of evaluation to include insights from parents and guardians, other adults or church members, coworkers, and pastors.

The key point here is that our uses of formative and summative evaluations reveal our desire for our youth ministry leadership and our youth ministry to be outcome rich. These means of evaluation show our intent not simply to carry out excellent hope-centered ministry, but to affirm how and to what extent we succeed in doing so.

✓CHECK IT OUT

Use the following questions to reflect on your operational aptitude. What would you say are your strengths as a decision maker and teacher? What would you say you need to work on? How would you describe your strengths as an administrator? How would you describe areas in need of change or improvement? What approaches to evaluation have you used? In what new ways may evaluation take place in your ministry with youth?

NOTES

1. Shawn A. Ginwright, *Black Youth Rising: Activism and Radical Healing in Urban America* (New York: Columbia Univ. Press, 2010), 155, confirms that there are no simple steps to solving the problems of black youth. He says, "Effective work with African American youth requires more than simply step-by-step recipes for success." Their situations did not unfold in easy 1, 2, 3 steps and cannot be addressed through recipe solutions.

2. Ron Taffel with Melinda Blau, *The Second Family: Dealing with Peer Power, Pop Culture, the Wall of Silence—and Other Challenges of Raising Today's Teens* (New York: St. Martin's, 2001), 49–51.

3. Ginwright writes of a Leadership Excellence (LE) program in California in which he found the same yearning of black urban youth to tell their stories. He states, "After years of trial and error, we learned at LE that youth rarely want or need to be talked at, but want to be listened to without judgment, which of course is very difficult when you deeply care about someone." Ginwright, *Black Youth Rising*, 69.

4. See Elizabeth Struthers Malbon, *In the Company of Jesus: Characters in Mark's Gospel* (Louisville: Westminster John Knox, 2000), 93–94.

5. Examples of story linking appear in Anne E. Streaty Wimberly, *Soul Stories: African American Christian Education*, rev. ed. (Nashville: Abingdon, 2005).

6. In the black church, these functions are carried out by the black preacher, but they are applicable to the role of the youth ministry leader as mentor. They are described in Anne E. Streaty Wimberly, *Nurturing Faith and Hope: Black Worship as a Model for Christian Education* (Cleveland: Pilgrim, 2004; repr., Eugene, OR: Wipf and Stock, 2010), 139–43.

7. Ginwright, *Black Youth Rising*, 68.

8. Seeing youth as a gift from God is presented as the first step forward to be taken by churches in the prologue of Anne E. Streaty Wimberly, ed., *Keep It Real: Working with Today's Black Youth* (Nashville: Abingdon, 2005), xix.

9. Na'ilah Suad Nasir, *Racialized Identities: Race and Achievement among African American Youth* (Stanford, CA: Stanford Univ. Press, 2012), 3, 30,

addresses the negative impact of media portrayals and stereotypes of black youth by saying that these images have implications for how they perceive themselves.

10. In the Vision Quest national telephone survey, leaders highlighted six primary ways of addressing youth program challenges. Listed in rank order according to the percentage of leaders' responses, these ways include: pray about it (96.9 percent); speak with parents (92.3 percent); speak with youth (90.0 percent); speak with pastoral staff (87.7 percent); speak with coworkers (78.5 percent); and seek help from advisory committee (71.5 percent). A very small number said they would either disregard or ignore the challenge (6.2 percent) or discontinue their leadership (6.2 percent).

4
Preparing for Hope-Centered Leadership

And we want each one of you to show the same diligence
so as to realize the full assurance of hope to the very end,
so that you may not become sluggish, but imitators of those
who through faith and patience inherit the promises.
—Hebrews 6:11-12

Imagine marathon runners positioned at a starting point, silent, excited, and anxious to get the race on. The silence is pierced by the words of the starter, "Get ready! Set!" then the cracking sound of the gun. With skill and every ounce of strength, will, and hope, runners race forward—up hills, down slopes, and around curves, stopping at designated points for nourishment and encouragement to continue on to the finish line. But there's a backstory: marathon runners prepare for months or years, doing research, finding a coach, obtaining the right gear, adhering to a balanced nutritional diet and hydration plan, training daily to develop strength and resilience. And embedded in every preparatory action is the inwardly stated arousal to action, "Let me be ready! Let me make good on my hope of crossing the finish line. Let me be prepared!"

Preparation for youth ministry leaders bears some resemblance to preparation for a marathon. As leaders, we must organize and expect to reach ministry goals, believe that our work will not be in vain, take full advantage of available resources, and confidently rely on spiritual nourishment that has its source in God.

Hope in God is the fuel that energizes youth ministry and propels us forward in the race. That hope begins with our call and vision. Scripture tells us that who God calls he equips (Hebrews 13:21). Some of our equipping for youth ministry will come from skills and talents we have acquired throughout our lives, some will come from ministry gifts that God bestows on us, and some will come through the hard work of study and serving in the church. All of these things work together to prepare us to educate, engage, and equip black youth.

In this chapter we will consider the nature of leaders' preparedness for hope-centered ministry. The Vision Quest national survey, visits to and observations of youth ministry leadership in congregations, and meetings with leaders gave us some important clues to this preparatory process and challenges to it. These clues come from information about who leads and what works and what does not work in preparing for effective leadership. They provide a perspective for reflection on our own leadership and preparation for it. The chapter explores these clues for the sake of helping us look at ourselves and answer these questions: What is the typical profile of a ministry leader with black youth today? Where do I fit in the profile? What is involved in leader preparation? What types of congregational spaces and support systems encourage and sustain leader preparedness? Which ones do I need right now or may I make happen?

This chapter also draws attention to limitations in preparation and to strategies that enhance leaders' abilities to be agents of hope. Look in this chapter as well for remedies and best practices for use in leadership preparation that takes into consideration church denomination, church size, geographic region, and leadership type. These aspects of leadership preparedness invite reflection by youth ministry leaders, educators, and observers on what may yet be needed to insure ongoing leadership readiness.

Some who read this chapter may be currently involved in youth ministry or be interested in entering this fulfilling, exciting vocation. What is included here is for you! Some may be helpers in leader preparation or teachers or mentors of those in some phase of preparedness. This chapter is for you too! Before continuing, consider the questions in the "Check It Out" section here.

✓CHECK IT OUT

What initial insights do you have about what is needed to prepare leaders for hope-centered ministry in the black church? What initial answers would you give to the questions: What is involved in leader preparation? What types of congregational spaces and support systems encourage and sustain leader preparedness? Which ones do I need right now or may I make happen?

Leadership Preparation in the Bible

Did you know that the word *prepare* is referenced more than a hundred times in the Bible? Although context varies, the word is used to challenge, exhort, and in some cases warn someone to plan for a future responsibility, opportunity, or problem. We know, for example, that God called Moses to deliver the Israelites out of Egypt. But Moses did not take on this responsibility without preparation. He gained leadership acumen over years in the desert and with the help of his father-in-law, Jethro. Moreover, critical preparation for his leadership role came from God. Joshua was Moses' assistant and was installed as leader after Moses' death. His preparation for his task of leading the Israelites into Canaan was advanced through his relationship with Moses, his mentor.[1]

The apostle Paul's prior studies under his mentor Gamaliel and his membership in the Sanhedrin gave him important tools when he became a leader for Christ after his transformation. The disciples prepared for leadership in Jesus' presence as they listened to and saw him unfold the principles of ministry. Their leadership formation continued by their putting the principles into practice. Their preparation was possible because they were teachable. They were devoted to Jesus, their Teacher and Model, and they were able and willing to give of themselves wholeheartedly in practicing what they learned.[2]

Inherent in the word *prepare* is the notion that there are some prerequisites leaders must satisfy. Moreover, it points to the importance of intentionality, strategic decision making, and readiness. In contrast, the lack of preparation is often associated with less than ideal outcomes, such as loss, inefficiency, frustration, and possibly defeat. Whether through schooling, experiential learning, mentorship, apprenticeship, or God's gifting, leadership preparation that is portrayed in the Bible, particularly in the New Testament, was for the following purposes:

- To develop leaders who have learned to follow
- To train within the context of personal apprenticeship
- To make a commitment to the community as well as training for a task
- To stress the spiritual aspects of leadership[3]

The Bible is full of examples that stress the centrality of preparedness. And we can learn from them as we consider what is required to be an effective leader of hope-centered youth ministry.

The Leaders, Their Preparation and Challenges

Youth ministry leaders in the Vision Quest study were of various adult ages, though most were younger in age and female. They had a range of experiences in and beyond youth ministry. Most were single, although the leaders include married individuals who, in most cases, did not have children who took part in the youth programs they lead. Most were formally educated, and some were seminary graduates or current seminarians. These leaders identified themselves as laypersons in churches, ordained youth pastors, ordained clergy, associate pastors, directors of Christian education, and simply as youth ministry leaders. Most interestingly, despite the educational backgrounds or other credentials, many of them were unpaid volunteers.

The important point here is that a significant number of youth ministry leaders in the Vision Quest study were educationally prepared. They were committed to their ministries, and they held several traits in common—love for God and youth and a desire to exhibit their love for both in youth ministry. They also exhibited great hope for youth and a readiness to move forward toward the finish line by impacting the lives of black youth.

✓CHECK IT OUT

For a moment, consider your profile. Recall alone or share with another leader or in a group of leaders the following topics:

- your age/stage

- your marital status

- any children in your family who are in your youth group

- your educational background and how that background prepared you for youth ministry leadership

- your youth ministry position title

- whether you are paid or are an unpaid volunteer

- your hope for moving toward the finish line

- your reflection on your preparedness to move forward in ministry or your willingness and availability to be a mentor or coach for someone else who is preparing for youth ministry leadership or desires leadership retooling

Although they have strong motivations, youth leaders may find themselves ill-prepared to carry out the tasks for which they have been called in their particular location. When this happens, their race forward is halted. Their hope gets short-circuited. This was the case with Karen, who told of becoming the pastor in a small church in a small town. Her role as youth ministry leader was added on to her pastoral role simply because no one seemed to want to take responsibility for the youth. She said, "I just have a passion for youth. Even though there aren't a lot of youth in my church, there's still a few; and there are a bunch of them in the neighborhood who don't go to anybody's church. I see kids in and outside the church with family issues, drug issues, violence issues, school issues. Something has to happen with them. I guess I'm it. I mean, I would like to do something about it." She continued, "But I'm not sure I'm up to the task! Sure, I'm seminary-trained. But it's going to take more than I learned in seminary. I've gotta have some help."

So, what is needed to prepare, become better prepared, or be retooled? How may preparedness come about along the way, especially in challenging situations? Where may leaders like Karen and others in comparable situations turn for help? How can they more proactively rather than reactively respond to limitations linked to people, places, and processes? Strategies and best practices can take many forms. Here we focus on those specifically related to leadership preparation, because the more prepared a youth ministry leader is, the more she or he can convert potential *obstacles* into ministry *opportunities* that move youth ministry forward with hope.

Pathways to Preparation

Taking advantage of formal and informal educational opportunities are at the heart of preparing for ministry with youth.

Formal pathways of preparation or retooling are of four types:

- *Formal educational institutions*, such as seminaries, Bible colleges, and other higher education institutions where degree programs, continuing education seminars, and youth worker certificate programs are found.

- *Denominationally sponsored* seminars or workshops focused on age/stage ministry, youth ministry, and Christian education for youth.

- *Youth worker conferences or seminars* sponsored by national organizations that often hold events in regional locations, such as the Congress on Urban Ministry meetings and the Seminary Consortium for Urban Pastoral Education (SCUPE) program in Chicago, Illinois; Urban Ministries, Inc. (UMI), workshops in Chicago; National Youth Workers Conventions, held in differing locations across the country throughout each year; Urban Youth Workers Institute (UYWI), which moves from city to city across the country; Urban Outreach Conference, annual meetings sponsored by Hope for the Inner City, Chattanooga, Tennessee; and Princeton Forums on Youth Ministry sponsored by Princeton Theological Seminary.

• *Podcasts and webinars*, such as those provided by the Youth Workers Conferences and the Princeton Forums on Youth Ministry.

Preparatory experiences in these settings provide structured face-to-face and sometimes distance-learning opportunities to gain knowledge, guidance, and teaching from experts in areas such as Christian education, church administration, Bible study, and teaching techniques to prepare or retool youth ministry leaders for their roles. Formal training is desirable because it expands one's overall knowledge base through concentrated, intentional exposure to a variety of subjects from persons specifically trained in these arenas.

To be well prepared, youth ministry leaders must reject a distrustful view of formal education that is common in some church settings. The church and the academy must inform each other with a focus on learning outcomes if youth leaders and their ministries are going to be well prepared. For example, seminaries are preparing students around issues of multidisciplinary teaching and ministry; nontraditional, creative youth evangelism through technology; effective youth ministry in urban, rural, suburban, and virtual contexts; specific techniques to teach potentially controversial subjects such as racism, classism, sexism, and sexuality; as well as practical, cross-cultural, reflective, and interdisciplinary methodologies for research, teaching, and service. These types of subjects represent contemporary areas of expertise youth ministry leaders should master to be best prepared.

Informal pathways of preparation or retooling offer special and personalized guidance and help that fit specific circumstances. They include the following:

- Facebook meetings and chat rooms.

- Person-to-person and intra- and inter-church mentoring or coaching by previous youth ministry leaders, senior pastors, other clergy and lay leaders who work with youth, and even church members who engage youth in their secular positions who have potentially helpful knowledge for youth ministry leaders.

- Magazines and journals, available through subscription and online, such as YouthMinistry.com; *YouthWorker Journal*, published bimonthly with subscriptions available at Youthworker.com; *YouthWorker eJournal*, and *Group Magazine*, with digital application, blogger network, e-books and resources at www.youthministry.com/group; and online subscriptions at www.groupmagazine.com.

These options offer a broad range of information for use in preparing effective youth ministry leaders. Vital leadership preparation requires a diverse information team at the disposal of leaders and to which they can refer for counsel and support. These informal means can also inform leaders about particular youth ministry challenges and/or limitations in black churches and communities that cannot be easily resolved or about alternative approaches that may be pursued.

These informal means are helpful, for example, in providing guidance and advice for use in running the youth ministry race. They may be used to proactively put out ministry crises; lovingly deal with disgruntled parents; provide structured, supportive direction to unchurched youth; offer ideas for addressing health, drug, gang, or school-related issues; meet the needs of a demographically diverse youth base, including urban, suburban, small town, and rural youth; brainstorm where to find needed human and economic resources for youth activities; provide hope during seemingly hopeless situations; and encourage needed personal rest and relaxation to prepare for the next spiritual marathon.

Because youth ministry leaders are mentors themselves, some may find it difficult to seek out mentors or coaches. Yet doing so is crucial, because a mentor or coach will be an invaluable sounding board to help sustain and support leaders spiritually, physically, emotionally, and psychologically. This point cannot be emphasized enough: youth ministry leaders must accept the reality that challenges will come and limitations are inevitable. Yet whether these potentially negative situations are considered obstacles or opportunities will often be determined by how well prepared a youth ministry leader is to address them.

✓ CHECK IT OUT

Take some time now either alone or with another leader or a group of leaders and reflect on your uses of pathways to preparation or retooling. What formal pathways to youth ministry preparation have you used? What kinds of help have you gained from the formal pathways? What informal pathways to youth ministry preparation have you used? What kinds of help have you gained from the informal pathways? What new formal and/or informal pathways to youth ministry preparation will you seek? Which ones would you use that were not mentioned?

Preparedness for Ongoing Ministry Requires Support

When youth ministry leaders are intentionally prepared, we're ready to take off when the Ultimate Starter says, "Ready! Set! Go!" But we know we will come to points along the way where we need sustenance and encouragement to go the course. Without supportive actions from within ourselves and from without, energies for the ministry diminish. Our sense of preparedness for all that needs to be done wanes. We need to know that we are not alone in those "up hills, down slopes, and around curves" times of ministry. Read Irena's story below, and then we'll consider some suggestions for mobilizing supporters to assure that help is on the way!

Irena's Story. Irena is the youth ministry leader at Liberty Baptist Church. A Christian for over twenty years, Irena was trained "in the trenches" of this medium-sized urban congregation. Because of her "training by fire," Irena has witnessed God's power and promises in the youth ministry; she also prides herself on being prepared as a youth ministry leader and prays for godly guidance and sustenance. About thirty-five youth, most from a nearby housing project, participate in Liberty's youth ministry. The kids are excited, but after seven years of single-handedly leading this ministry, Irena is running out of steam. Volunteers have come and gone. Parents started out excited about their children's involvement but now seem to rely on Irena for everything from personal shuttle services to food preparation to free counseling—in addition to her roles as teacher and youth ministry organizer.

Most of Irena's challenges come from *inside* the church, as disgruntled elderly members express concerns about "those children" from the housing project. Irena's "come as you are" stance regarding the youths' attire, and her request for more money to fund youth ministry activities have become increasing bones of contention in the congregation. The pastor is noticeably silent about these complaints and unresponsive to Irena's continued requests for help. Sometimes Irena wants to quit. But the youth keep coming! They love Irena, and she loves them! The excited expressions on their faces, their continued queries about God and God's plan for their lives, and their optimism for the future despite their impoverished home lives are the only things sustaining her.

"Keep hope alive!" Irena jokingly recalls this common phrase. How can she remain hopeful for the hope-filled youth who have found a home in this ministry and despite the hope-draining church environment in which it takes place? What should Irena do? What people and processes should be in place to provide help along the way for leaders like Irena? What strategies and support can be given to undergird and empower leaders' ongoing preparedness for ministry?

Participants in the Vision Quest project gave some essential information in the form of six dynamics for assuring necessary support and ongoing preparedness of leaders. They include the following:

1. prayer
2. parents

3. pupils

4. pastoral staff

5. parishioners

6. practices

Remembering these six Ps will not simply help cultivate spaces of care for propping up leaders' preparedness. These dynamics will heighten the hope of leaders and others on which youth ministry in our churches centers. Leaders in the Vision Quest project said clearly that, rather than ignore challenges, discontinue leadership, or abandon hope, they in tandem with the actions of others successfully built up their ongoing preparedness for hope-centered ministry by addressing these six Ps. Four of the six Ps—prayer, parents, pupils, and pastoral staff—represent opportunities that leaders have taken upon themselves to address challenges. They are as follows:

Pray about It	96.9%
Speak with Parents	92.3%
Speak with Pupils	90.0%
Speak with Pastoral Staff	87.7%

Note the percentage of leaders who engaged in the spiritual practice of prayer. This means that when confronted by a problem occurring in youth ministry, almost all of the leaders who participated in Vision Quest said that prayer is a frontline action of assuring preparedness when the going gets tough! It was clear, too, that the nature of the problem, church size, church financial status, leadership role, denominational affiliation, number of youth or youth programs, or church sponsors didn't matter. They gave a powerful piece of advice based on their experience that prayer changes things! It also reminds us that both our preparedness and our hope can be renewed as we pray to God for consolation, clarity, and strength.

Of course, after prayer, more practical steps should be taken. The leaders made clear that contact with parents, followed by pupils/youth themselves and pastors are key approaches to addressing challenges. The order of contact is not as important as the need to do so, because each person in this tripartite network has some influence on the existence and effectiveness of youth ministry. Youth have influence in terms of participation, parents in terms of support, and pastors and other church leaders in terms of enlisting congregational leadership, guidance, and ministry sanctioning. The leaders highlighted the particular role of pastors. More than 90 percent said that pastors must be willing to support youth programs and adapt them to meet challenges and the needs of youth.

We must not leave out the remaining two Ps—parishioners and practices. In the national survey, leaders were asked to rate the importance of the congregation's support of the youth ministry leader and the congregation's sense of excitement about youth programs. In addition, participants in Vision Quest-sponsored youth ministry meetings were asked to comment on the congregational environment in which youth ministry takes place. Ninety percent of the national study participants indicated that "the congregation's support of the youth leader is very important" and an equal percentage said that it was "imperative that members of the congregation have a sense of excitement about youth programs."

Participants in meetings were quick to say that "the attitudes of parishioners toward youth and the level of their support of youth ministry and its leaders can literally make or break the ministry." In short, the study participants were adamant about the importance of parishioners being on the cheering line for youth ministry and those who lead it. Participants also commented that it is important for parishioners to encourage and support leaders' spiritual growth by standing up for opportunities that contribute to the spiritual nurture of these leaders. This may mean, for example, assuring and supporting leaders' time off and time apart for spiritual renewal, revival, and replenishment needed for forward preparedness and movement. Indeed, more than half of the youth ministry leaders in Vision Quest clearly pointed out the need for congregations to develop ways to prevent youth ministry leader burnout, create excitement about youth programs, and cultivate a clear vision for youth ministry.[4]

Practices are approaches or methods used to get a desired result. In youth ministry, helpful practices spell the difference in the leaders' preparedness for ongoing hope-centered ministry. The insights of leaders in the Vision Quest study tell us that teamwork is among the best approaches to build and assure youth ministry leaders' ongoing preparedness and hope-centered ministry. They were clear that successful youth ministry happens when there is a unified, stellar youth ministry leadership team that espouses a common vision and is upheld by a supportive pastoral team. Here are some of their comments:

- "Excellent youth ministry leadership happens when a team of persons are in sync with each other and share the same vision for youth ministry. It also takes a team that yields to God's desire for ministry that makes a difference in the lives of the youth, communicates this desire to the youth, and makes that ministry happen." (Leader in an AME church in Georgia)

- "Teamwork happens when you have a pastor that supports the vision of the youth leader/pastor and does not handicap him/her. But, leadership isn't carried out single-handed by the youth ministry leader. It requires a team that agrees on and seeks to carry out a vision and a mission for the youth to grow spiritually, physically, and mentally in God's Word." (Leader in an AME church in Florida)

- "[A prepared youth ministry leader must have] respect for pastoral leadership and affirmation of the vision, be able to plan and implement, understand the importance of a team effort, and [be] willing to lead by example. . . . [The leader] knows how to communicate with and motivate young people." (Leader in a Presbyterian church in South Carolina)

These remarks remind us of both the people and practices that can enhance hope-centered youth ministry and without which ministry may be undermined. The critical point is also that effective youth ministry leadership requires preparation before the starting line and ongoing preparedness along the way. But leaders must also be embedded in church environments that support our efforts.

Team efforts must be reflected in congregational and pastoral supportive practices. And pastors must take the lead! These practices include telling within and beyond the church about our youths' stories, their needs, and the ministry with them we cannot afford to forsake. Really, it is all about seeing the need, owning the responsibility, and pledging to make the ministry happen. The centrality of this requirement was reinforced by Vision Quest participants. Regardless of church size, denomination, or region, leaders said that this team imperative is a compelling factor in keeping youth ministry leaders committed to their roles.

In Irena's case, her youth ministry challenges are not the result of an absence of prayer on her part or lack of youth interest. She is a prayer warrior! She needs a team: parents who fully understand the purpose of youth ministry and their place in facilitating it and Irena's success; proactive support from the pastor and other church clergy; and a clearly defined youth ministry vision that includes practices for leadership renewal and growth, teambuilding, and excitement. When churches intentionally and proactively provide support for hope-centered youth ministry, they help insure that the many prepared youth ministry leaders like Irena can remain on their posts, secure in the knowledge that they are sanctioned by God and supported by youth, parents, clergy, and the overall congregation.

A Closing Word: Following Christ's Lead

Consider again the earlier reference to Jesus' concern about teaching and preparing the disciples to continue the work of spreading the Good News upon his departure. The New Testament is full of examples of how Jesus directly and indirectly preached, taught, and modeled godly living for his eager but often unprepared disciples. The disciples were fortunate pupils because they were receiving instruction from the Master Teacher. No one could have been more prepared than Christ. And because he was prepared, he could in turn prepare his disciples for what lay ahead. The role of youth ministry leader is not much different. The thought may come to us,

How can I be expected to be as prepared as the all-perfect Christ? The truth is that we are not expected to be perfect. Yet the model of Christ provides the perfect rubric for us (and other interested persons) to examine what we did to prepare and the level of our ongoing preparedness for youth ministry. Based on what we have learned thus far, and using the following acronyms, let's consider how youth ministry leaders may use Jesus' model to stay in touch with what it means to *PREPARE* and pay attention to continual *PREPAREDNESS.*

• **P**roactive—Because he knew he was moving toward Jerusalem to make the ultimate sacrifice, Christ was constantly making decisions in anticipation of his death (see John 13:1). Jesus knew he had only so long to preach, teach, and heal the masses as well as train the disciples. This type of leadership and decision making required great discernment and foresight to plan for future needs, problems, and change. Moreover, proactive youth ministry leadership means using past learning and experiences to thoughtfully plan future endeavors.

• **R**esponsible—Christ took responsibility for his earthly calling. Scripture documents some of his responsibilities (see Matthew 16:23; 18:11; and John 14:2-3 for examples). He embraced these tasks because he knew that no one else could perform them. Although being responsible can seem like a burden at times, Christ readily welcomed his role out of love for God and humanity. And by doing do, he was accountable to God for God's precious creation. Similarly, youth ministry leaders are answerable to God for the special young charges placed in their care. The responsibility may sometimes seem daunting, but God trusts such leaders to do their best.

• **E**ducated—As God in the flesh, Christ knew everything. He knew the thoughts, beliefs, concerns, and motives of everyone around him (see Matthew 12:25; Mark 8:17; John 6:61; and 13:1 for examples). Of course, youth ministry leaders will not. But youth ministry leaders are challenged to learn as much as possible. Learning can occur in various venues. Some will be blessed enough to get formal training at a seminary, Bible college, or through sanctioned online courses. Others may learn via Christian education conferences, local workshops, and church-sponsored training events. It is important that youth ministry leaders have biblical knowledge as well as practical strategies and approaches to attract and retain youth, meet their varied needs, and help them successfully negotiate life in their culture. We cannot educate youth if we are not educated ourselves.

• **P**lanning—Christ's conversation with the disciples in John 14:1-4 illustrates both planning and proactivity. Just as his entrance into the world was foretold in the Old Testament, Jesus' departure was required. After performing his earthly calling excellently, Christ informed the disciples with comforting words that he was leaving to prepare a heavenly place for them. This passage alludes to several examples of stellar planning. Christ's entire time on earth was a result of godly planning. Jesus had to plan in order to maximize his limited time on earth, and this passage illustrates that his planning as the Model Leader even extended into the heavenly realm! As youth ministry leaders, our plans may not be as magnificent as Christ's, but they are crucial, because youth ministry leaders are responsible for planning ministry that has the potential to transform lives. This requires intentionality, goal setting, organizational skills, follow-through, team building, procedural know-how, accountability, measurable outcomes, strategies, and contingency arrangements to best choreograph and maintain effective ministry.

• **A**ware—Matthew 12:13-17 illustrates Jesus' omniscience. He knew who needed his help. He also knew that the Pharisees were conspiring against him. Although Christ was aware of the latter negative plot for his demise, he was compelled by the former appeals—and responded miraculously. Christ was also aware that his reputation was growing. Each of these examples of cognition informed his attitudes and actions as a prepared leader. Jesus prepared for his life's ministry as he simultaneously prepared for his death. Broadly applying these truths means that prepared youth ministry leaders must be cognizant and discerning about the needs and desires of the youth in their charge. They must also be aware of available resources, potential roadblocks to ministry, existing assets, and untapped resources inside and outside church walls. Of equal importance, youth ministry leaders must be aware of their own personal needs, abilities, strengths, and breaking points so that they too are ready, willing, and able to lead.

• **R**esourceful—Some of the most engaging biblical stories focus on Christ's ability to make something out of nothing. Feeding the four thousand (Matthew 15:32-36) exemplifies this kind of resourcefulness. We often focus on the miraculous nature of this episode, but there is another more practical dimension to the story. We know that Christ could have merely spoken and the needed food would have appeared. However, he chose a more temporal way to feed the people, both spiritually and physically. He chose an approach that would remind people of how they could harness God's power to transform everyday things they already had at their disposal into life-changing resources. A prepared youth ministry leader must believe that he or she is capable of devising ways to meet the needs of youth in a given situation and then strategically and thoughtfully do so—often with limited resources. This means looking around at the human and nonhuman resources available for use in feeding youth.

• **E**mpowered—A prepared youth ministry leader needs godly power! Christians are already blessed with the indwelling of the Holy Spirit. But how often do leaders tap into that source of power during youth ministry? How often does that power source energize and reenergize leaders physically, spiritually, emotionally, and psychologically to continue in ministry? In Matthew 4:18-20, Christ promised the disciples that they would have power to be fishers of people. He promised them that his ecclesiastical authority would transfer to them and enable them to continue preaching, teaching, and healing. Effective youth ministry leaders must remember and rely on this promise of godly power.

The above biblical examples are only a few from a litany of ways Jesus Christ represents the ideal prepared leader. Furthermore, these ways to prepare and pay attention to ongoing preparedness are more than a play on words. They represent a model to emulate. Scripture also tells us that as followers of Christ, we will be able to

Chart 4.1. Preparation Assessment Guide

Triumphs	Trials	The Way Forward
Think about what you do, how you do it, and what motivates you. Also reflect on those times you have felt most prepared for youth ministry. Select one event that gave you a sense of preparedness and answer the following questions: • What was the event (e.g., Youth Sunday, a community youth picnic, a youth Bible study series, or a youth sleepover)? • Why did you feel prepared? • What types of things did you do to prepare for that event? • Did you prepare as a team or alone? • How did you feel after the event was over (e.g., what gave you a sense of great accomplishment)?	Reflect on those times you have felt least prepared for youth ministry. Select one event and answer the following questions: • What was the event (e.g., Youth Sunday, a community youth picnic, a youth Bible study series, or a youth sleepover)? • Why did you feel unprepared? • What types of things did you do to prepare for this event? • What "fell through the cracks"? • Did you prepare as a team or alone? • Do you think the challenges were due to your decision making or those of other people? Why? • How did you feel after the event was over (e.g., did you feel embarrassed, angry, disappointed, frustrated, ambivalent, and/or just exhausted)?	What did you learn from this chapter that has helped you better understand why you felt most prepared for the particular event you recalled under "Triumphs"? What did you learn from this chapter that has helped you better understand why you felt least prepared for the particular event you named under "Trials"? Write down your responses and look for identifiable insights. • Jot down patterns that emerged. • Recollect processes, people, other resources, as well as personal attitudes and actions that resulted in your feeling prepared. • Also recollect processes, people, other resources, as well as personal attitudes and actions that you now believe have undermined experiences of preparedness. • Reflect on ways these instances of recall can illumine your pathway forward.

do more than he did (John 14:12). This is the assurance that when youth ministry leaders give our all to this great ministry, success will follow. We are challenged to be as prepared as Christ was and allow God's power and provisions to do the rest.

Now, alone or sharing with others, use the Preparation Assessment Guide on the previous page to reflect on your role as a youth ministry leader and your preparation for it. Return to this guide at various points in your youth ministry leadership journey. Assessing your experiences of preparedness along the way is to uncover processes, people, other resources, personal thoughts, and decisions that will be helpful as you continue on. Know that recalling those times of ill preparation is just as important as recalling the most satisfying ones, because that recall invites consideration of strategies that can help you avoid repeating bad practices as you carry on hope-centered youth ministry leadership. Documenting, praying about, and replicating the dynamics you have entered into in this assessment are important! Enter into moments of prayer now.

Resources

The following sources provide helpful insights for preparing for youth ministry leadership and ongoing preparedness.

Barnes, Sandra. *Black Megachurch Culture: Models for Education and Empowerment*. New York: Peter Lang, 2010.

_____. "Religion and Rap Music: An Analysis of Black Church Usage." *Review of Religious Research* 49, no. 3 (2009): 319–38.

Billingsley, Andrew. *Climbing Jacob's Ladder: The Enduring Legacy of African-American Families*. New York: Touchstone, 1992.

Cook, Kaye V. "You Have to Have Somebody Watching Your Back, and If That's God, Then That's Mighty Big: The Church's Role in the Resilience of Inner-City Youth." *Adolescence* 35, no. 140 (2000): 717–30.

DuBois, W. E. Burghardt. Ed. *The Negro Church*. Report of a Social Study made under the Direction of Atlanta University; Together with the Proceedings of the Eighth Conference for the Study of the Negro Problems, held at Atlanta University, May 26, 1903. Atlanta: Atlanta University Press, 1903. Reprinted: Walnut Creek, CA: Altimira, 1989; and Eugene, OR: Cascade Books, an imprint of Wipf and Stock Publishers, 2011.

Hill, Johnny B. Ed. *Multidimensional Ministry for Today's Black Family.* Valley Forge, PA: Judson Press, 2007.

Lincoln, C. Eric, and Lawrence H. Mamiya. *The Black Church in the African-American Experience.* Durham, NC: Duke Univ. Press, 1990.

Mays, Benjamin, and Joseph W. Nicholson. *The Negro's Church.* New York: Institute of Social and Religious Research, 1933.

Watkins, Ralph C. *The Gospel Remix: Reaching the Hip Hop Generation.* Valley Forge, PA: Judson Press, 2007.

West, Cornel. *Race Matters.* Boston: Beacon, 1993.

Wimberly, Anne E. Streaty. *Keep It Real: Working with Today's Black Youth.* Nashville: Abingdon, 2005.

NOTES

1. Leopold A. Foullah, "The Preparation for Leadership," http://ezinearticles.com/?The-Preparation--for-Leadership, accessed October 3, 2012.

2. See Barry McWilliams, "Jesus' Leadership Principles and Method of Training His Disciples," www.eldrbarry.net/ug/8and7.pdf.

3. See Foullah, "Preparation for Leadership," who drew the material from David W. Bennett, *Leadership Images from the New Testament: A Practical Guide* (Carlisle, UK: OM Publishing, 1998), 33–34.

4. Findings from the Vision Quest National Survey showed that about 62 percent of Baptists believe their churches have a clear vision of youth ministry: 50.4 percent of churches in the Midwest believe the same.

PART 2

Hope-Centered Youth Ministry

Pay close attention to yourself and your teaching;
continue in these things, for in doing this
you will save both yourself and your hearers.
—1 Timothy 4:16

5

WELCOME MATTERS

Seeing, Reaching, and Hearing Youth

The people brought children to Jesus, hoping he might touch them. The disciples shooed them off. But Jesus was irate and let them know it: "Don't push these children away. Don't ever get between them and me. These children are at the very center of life in the kingdom. Mark this: Unless you accept God's kingdom in the simplicity of a child, you'll never get in." Then, gathering the children up in his arms, he laid his hands of blessing on them.
—Mark 10:13-16 (MSG)

The well-known Bible passage cited above provides keen insight into Jesus' views about youth. He considers their worth inestimable! In a society controlled by adults that typically rewards age, experience, and other traits associated with the length of one's existence, Jesus has a radical message: if you want to be accepted by God, be more like children. What a revolutionary message this is—and one that we should apply every day. People often think about youth in unfavorable ways—spoiled, bratty, illogical, whiny, rebellious, or silly. But this is not how Jesus sees them. He sees their hearts, their purity, honesty, vulnerability, and trusting nature. And these are types of characteristics Jesus wants all of us to express. This lesson from the Gospel of Mark can also be applied to the plans, processes, and programs needed to foster hope-filled youth ministry leaders that, by definition, must master the ability to effectively *see*, *reach*, and *hear* our youth.

In this chapter we will explore the matter of seeing, reaching, and hearing youth from various perspectives. What we are really about here is *hospitality*, a practice that refers to our ability to be genuinely gracious, sociable, generous, and cordial as we receive someone into our presence. Hospitality requires us to welcome people as valuable guests as we intentionally create an environment that makes them feel at home! Hospitable youth ministry quickly makes youth feel like family members to those who lead them and to the whole congregation!

Also in this chapter, we will give attention to a wide range of programs and activities that are designed to see, reach, and hear our youth for the purpose of promoting their claiming and acting on their unapologetic Christian identity and unashamed black identity. As we begin, consider: What do we see when a youth comes into our presence, our youth group, or our church? How do we reach that person? What does listening have to do with it? Let's keep these questions in mind as we move forward. And let's agree that the starting point is *seeing* our youth.

Sawubona ("I See You")

In a Vision Quest workshop, parents and youth began with an introductory activity that included a Zulu greeting in South Africa, *Sawubona* ("I see you"), to acknowledge a person's presence from across the room. The response was, *Sikhona* or *Ngikhona* ("I am here"), to affirm the acknowledgment. This verbal exchange had a twofold meaning. The greeting verified one another's existence. It was an acknowledgment of the Zulu folk saying that "A person is a person because of other people." The response is acknowledgment on the part of persons that they are recognized and know themselves as connected to others.

But more than this, the greeting and response meant that *seeing someone embodies all of who they are*. In fact, it acknowledges all that is part of the developmental characteristics of youth appearing in chapter 2. We saw in that chapter that leadership up close and personal with youth means recognizing

111

that, like us, our youth exist as physical, emotional, intellectual, social, contextual, cultural, and spiritual beings. According to a graduation speech given by a teen, *Sawubona* means "Not only do I see you; I see all that you are—your personality, your humanity, and your dignity—and I respect what I see."[1] Being seen and knowing we are seen creates a welcoming space for open conversation. Incorporating this form of greeting in youth ministry also draws attention to our African heritage and what may be learned from it.

The importance of seeing and being seen encompasses a tremendous amount of what it means to welcome our youth into youth ministry. Seeing and welcoming go together! Seeing them becomes connected with welcoming actions. Seeing our youth means that ministry leaders and the whole congregation cultivate youth ministries that creatively and thoughtfully embrace dynamics that *include*, *affirm*, *stretch*, and *deepen* the lives of youth in the congregation and community.[2] How do we do it?

- We *include* youth as *active participants in worship* that speaks to them; and we assure places for them to meet, have a voice, and serve.

- We *affirm* youth as *valuable creations of God*, indispensable members of our intergenerational "village," and contributors to the life of today's and tomorrow's church and world. We affirm them as young, gifted, and black persons.

- We *stretch* youth's understanding of who and Whose they are by offering them educational, spiritual, leadership, service, and recreational opportunities that explore their cultural history, the Christian life, meanings of Christian discipleship, and their life purpose.

- We *deepen* youth's spiritual lives and resolve to follow Jesus Christ by our modeling the Christian life before them, being prayer warriors with them and on their behalf, engaging them in Bible study and other spiritual disciplines, and being present with them in their daily walk in readiness to pick them up when they fall and not give up on them.

We who are called to youth ministry and those in congrega
tions where this ministry takes place have the awesome task of
seeing all of who our youth are and what will build them up and
make possible their surviving and thriving in what often is a rough
world. But most of today's youth reside in a "gated community"
of youth-isms, guarded against those who endeavor to enter their
space. Their language is different, their dress is different, and what
some youth call their "swag" or unique way of walking or moving
about is different from previous generations and will likely change
again. Studies show that many black churches are having difficulty
attracting and retaining youth.[3] Yet churches that are intentionally
incorporating Christian hip-hop or holy hip-hop by artists such
as GRITS, Gospel Gangstaz, and Rev. Run are making headway
with youth. Access to information via technology such as Internet
browsers and Facebook expose youth to subjects and experiences
that most adults were not cognizant of when we were their age (see
more in chapter 6).

We have also been reminded previously that, to some youth,
adults are out of touch with their reality. In fact, Christian adults
are often considered the most outdated and antiquated of adults.
Given the seemingly expansive chasm between today's techno-savvy
youth and their parents and other adults, the task of seeing youth
can be daunting. This means that the ability to reach them can be
easily thwarted if the appropriate people, processes, and programs
are not in place. And if we do not reach out to them, there is little
chance that we will be in a position to hear them. But youth ministry leaders and churches seeking to have a vital youth ministry are
challenged to get it right. We have to first see our youth!

We mentioned in previous chapters that a chasm often exists
between youth in our churches and unchurched youth. Yet there
are places where this chasm is bridged. Tess, a Vision Quest survey
participant, told about her unchurched youths' unreadiness for the
church and the church's unreadiness for them. She struck an agreement with the pastor to work with the youth and the congregation
separately to get each group ready to be together. She altered her
appearance to look more like the youth in her charge because it

granted her entrance into their gated community. She continued to work with the youth and church members until she was able to build bridges needed for connection across the two groups. She was successful because both groups "saw her" as an ally willing to make sacrifices to work with them. Her dedication, honesty, and transparency resulted in the church's seeing and welcoming the youth and the youth seeing and welcoming the church members.

Youth ministry leaders and churches seeking to have a vital youth ministry are challenged to get it right. We have to see our youth. And, yes, church folk and youth must be able to see each other.

✓CHECK IT OUT

Consider at this point the questions that were raised earlier. What do you *see* when you look at youth? Go a step further. How does your church reach youth? How did your seeing them make a difference in what you did to reach out to them? How has seeing them guided your efforts to hear them? Consider what is done in your church to include, affirm, stretch, and deepen the lives of youth in and outside your church doors.

Imagine a Sawubona Church

Getting an image of what a *Sawubona* church looks like builds on our responses to the above questions. But let's stretch ourselves a bit further. We said in an earlier chapter that up-close, face-to-face relationships are necessary in our age of distant connections by social media. Although persons may welcome the text messages they receive and even delight in seeing family or friends on Skype, it is not the same as being in the same space. The welcoming space is where eye contact exists and is not avoided between adults and youth and among youth. The welcoming space is where the eyes, our spiritual eyes, perceive a youth to be God's child—our child. When we perceive youth in this way, our eyes communicate the reverence and love we have for youth, and this look is matched by how we treat them. What we see and perceive with our eyes connects with the kind of care we give or don't give. In other words, youth know from a glance if they are accepted and if we have a desire to include and care for them. In fact, an African proverb says that because of all that is communicated by the eyes, "seeing is better than hearing." Eyes often talk before actions speak.

A story from one youth in Tennessee reflects a church's welcome and how the congregation saw the youth: "I was basically coming to church on Sunday only because I spent the night with friends on Saturday. So when I first came here, they were very loving. They care about you. Basically they don't look at you like an ordinary person off the street. It's like you're family when you come here. So it was very lovable when I came here."

Imagine creating such a loving and welcoming church that youth in neighboring communities strategize how to come to church on Sunday. The above example illustrates what the congregation saw—a youth who was more than ordinary, a youth who was seen and accepted as family.

Build a Sawubona Church

If we are to succeed in having a *Sawubona* church, then we must be proactive about it. We need some concrete ideas for making it happen. Youth ministry leaders in the Vision Quest project confess that it isn't always easy. But it's necessary, and you have to keep on it! So what may we do to build a *Sawubona* church? Some of the tips they gave are as follows:

Visualize It

For example, said Mike, "We saw a lot of our young guys out on the street and not in the church. So we thought about a football field and seeing the guys on the football field. They are all at different positions. Some are on the 10 yard line, some are on the 50. But still others are on the sidelines and haven't gotten on the field at all. Maybe they haven't been invited; maybe they think they aren't good enough. Maybe they just don't like football or don't feature themselves in a football game. But still, it was a way of seeing where we wanted them and where we thought God was trying to move them. So we started an End Zone ministry for young men, and we let them take over. The church was all for it. What we envisioned was God and us as God's hands trying to move them from wherever they were to the end zone, which represents the abundant life of hope, love, and peace that Christ died for all of us to have. No, they didn't come in big numbers at first. But what we visualized did happen. At one of the meetings, one guy talked about how glad he was to be there. This was important because he was invited by one of the dads in the church. The vision we had was important. What we did to make it happen was important because sometimes we are all these kids really have."

Make the Vision Plain for All to See

In Habakkuk 2:2, God replies to the prophet, who is standing at the watch post waiting for an answer, "Write the vision; make it plain on tablets, so that a runner may read it." This became a guide for a youth ministry leader who was increasingly bothered by seeing the age segregation in the congregation. Marcie said, "The adults were separated from the youth, the youth separated from the children. Choir kids hung out with choir kids. Adults were in the sanctuary, the youth in the youth house, and the children in children's church. We came up with a vision for a praise café with youth in mind but open for everybody. We wrote it down, presented it, and got it approved. Youth signed up to present spoken word, dance, stepping. Even some of the adults presented. We called it praise café because we wanted everybody to see that you can praise God in many ways. The parents came to support the kids. The elders came because there was food. Everybody came to see what was going on. It became a multigenerational function where everybody had a part."

Reclaim Old Visions

In some instances, separate youth worship takes youth away from intergenerational communal rituals that open the way for their accepting and claiming their place in the community, their calling, and being affirmed for it. One of the Vision Quest study meetings brought youth ministry leaders, parents, and youth together. Ted, the father of one of the teens, stood and recalled when he was a teen: "Everyone had to walk to the front of the church on their own to give their life to Christ. Well, every one of us youth dreaded that day when the Lord was going to speak to you. So we had a confirmation class, and we could all join church together. That was important to me. On the day my group went forward, the pastor said two things that were important to me. First, 'God has a calling on your lives,' and second, 'God has a plan for your lives.' An older adult stood and said to the youth, 'You are all special. You have gifts that God has given you. We love you, and we want you to make good on your gifts. We have high expectations for you. Let us know what we can do to help.' I realized at that moment that I was not the dummy that I had convinced myself that I was. My parents were there for me. The church was there for me." As Ted sat down, participants across the room shouted, "Amen!" The message was that seeing our youth *with* us, and telling them of the promise of God's activity in their lives, cannot be ignored. A response to the testimony was, "We're going to have to bring back some of things we've had in the past. We need all of that stuff Ted talked about if our youth and all of us are going to survive."

Let Go of Some Visions

In our churches and in our youth ministry, we are here in the spirit of Jesus, "not to be served but to serve" (Matthew 20:28). So how are we doing as a church[4] and in our youth ministry? Consider for a moment the relationship between Paul and Timothy in Acts 16. Although Paul is a seasoned apostle and missionary as compared to Timothy, he does not consider Timothy to be merely a young man in need of being saved and included in a missionary "count" of success stories. No, Paul wanted Timothy to be involved in the church as a leader in his own right. Paul was clearly interested in Timothy's own transformation as well as in his potential for leadership.[5] What guidance does this give us in our relationship with today's youth?

Many churches today are experiencing an exodus of youth. Yet our youth are crying out to be seen and to be seen completely rather than to be thought of as a number to "grow" a ministry. There is a tendency in our day to pile on activities and fun-and-game endeavors to draw youth and keep them active without going beyond these activities. We fail to see the youth and to select activities that build a "seeing-one-another community," which leads to hearing them and tending to their stories. Sure, we want to grow our youth groups and our churches, but let's be intentional about seeing, including, affirming, stretching, and deepening the youth we have, however few they may be.

Building a *Sawubona* church and youth ministry means that we take to heart the joy of welcoming our youth. It means choosing to see them, knowing that if we really see them, we will reach them and be ready to hear them. This is the welcoming way. We want youth to know they are received and seen in a way that they can honestly relate back to us the meaning of *Sikhona*, "I am here."

✓CHECK IT OUT

In what ways would you enhance your spiritual sight to create more welcoming spaces for youth? What personal challenges do you face that undermine your ability to clearly "see" youth and create youth ministry that includes, affirms, stretches, and deepens their lives? What is yet needed for your congregation to become a *Sawubona* church?

Reaching Youth

In chapter 3, we gave much attention to ways of connecting with youth. The chapter emphasized that leaders make real connections with youth when they reach them where they are, invite youths' reaching back, bridge the gap between churched and unchurched youth, and give youth opportunities to connect with other youth. The following story from an interview with a youth in The Vision Quest study shows what can happen when the connection is made and youth reach back.

"I was not raised in church, but this girl invited us to her youth group. This was something to do on a Thursday night to keep off the street. So we went, and they said we would have to come to church two Sundays a month to participate in the youth group. So we agreed. We met a woman named Barbara, and she became like a mother to all of us. We felt that we could talk to her about anything. It was cool because we didn't think she was trying to indoctrinate us with all that religious stuff. We loved it. We became a group of kids who went to church two Sundays a month. We wanted to know what church was and what was this place? She saw us for who we were. She listened to us. She didn't judge us. The way she treated us made a huge difference. One time they had a youth revival. They had this guy preach, and he was only fifteen years old. He looked like us. He talked like us, and he explained things in a way that we got it. That particular night we all joined the church. Some of our parents came for the first time to see what church was all about."

Excellent and hope-centered youth ministry includes experiences that result in youths' saying, "This is the place for me!" Or, as a youth said in an interview, "No matter who you are, or where you come from, and no matter what others think of you, when you come in, you are welcomed with open arms; and they try to get you into the ministry as fast as possible. They want you to be there." These experiences extend to relevant programs and activities that help youth dig into and make sense out of the stories they live every day. Moreover, a hope-centered agenda targets youths' discovery of content and meanings of the Christian faith that give them handles on how faith connects with their present and future lives. How we make this agenda happen is important! Goal setting begins this kind of program development process.

Set Worthy Ministry Goals

A helpful way of considering goals is to take renewed notice of the characteristics of youth in our youth ministry and ones we seek to reach. When we take seriously these characteristics, we also make holistic ministry central. Include goals of spiritual development, cultural awareness and affirmation, social learning, environmental and political awareness and response, cognitive development and

Chart 5.1. Youth Ministry Goals

Youth Ministry Goals	Goal Description
Spiritual Development	• Develop youth ministry that contributes to youths' spiritual formation. • Make it Christ-centered, and link the Bible and Christian values with Christian living. • Engage youth in examining and practicing meanings of Christian discipleship and vocation, and expose them to church and denominational history and beliefs.
Cultural Awareness and Affirmation	• Develop youth ministry that contributes to black youths' seeing themselves as unashamed black persons and their bodies as gifts and temples of God. • Create opportunities that increase black youths' awareness of black history, its importance for their views of themselves, and reasons for activism past and present. This ministry also gives attention to ethnic cultural arts expression.
Social Learning	• Develop youth ministry that supports youths' social-relational development. • Place youth with adults so that they learn ways of serving with and apart from adults in and beyond the church. • Focus attention on how Christians relate with one another and with others across denominations and cultures in the everyday world. • Engage youth in actions that advance youths' understanding of working together for one another's and others' good.
Environmental and Political Awareness and Response	• Create opportunities for youth to share their everyday stories about home, school, church, and community. • Invite observation and awareness of local and global affairs and needs for community service. • Engage youth in critical reflection on how their stories and observations inform their feelings, attitudes, and understandings of Christian faith and action.
Cognitive Development and Educational Preparedness	• In every aspect of youth ministry, create opportunities for youth to think about, reflect on, offer ideas, and plan courses of action based on the values and norms of the Christian faith. • Stress the importance of education and work/vocational preparedness.
Emotional Well-Being	• Develop youth ministry that contributes to youths' positive identity formation, resilience, and embrace of a future of hope for themselves based on the Christian faith. • Engage youth in activities that help them look critically at their self-perceptions. Focus on key teen issues, problem-solving, conflict resolution, and activities that help them explore grief and anger.
Physical Development	• Offer activities that take into account differences in youths' physical development, including confronting physical challenges. • Create open discussion about health issues, care of self, sex, and sexuality.

educational preparedness, emotional well-being, and physical development as in chart 5.1.

Achieve Ministry Goals

A range of programs and activities that carry out youth ministry goals are possible in small, medium-sized, or large churches and regardless of location. However, according to youth ministry leaders across the country, choices of what exactly to do or how much is possible depends on available material resources such as facilities, materials and supplies, and equipment. These decisions also rely on relational resources such as parental, volunteer, and congregational support. But even when material and relational resources are unavailable or in short supply, getting programs and activities started that meet identified goals can happen because excitement is generated by youth ministry leaders and youth to do it. Together they have an idea whose time has come or a program or activity that must take place. And they hold to the idea that they can and will get it done! Their zest or enthusiasm and belief in their ability to do it are called *ideational resources*.[6] When this excitement spills over to include pastors or other church officials and parents, there is no stopping the momentum forward. In fact, when this kind of ideational resource emerges, relational and material resources are likely to follow. This was the case in the earlier story of the praise café. Choices of programs and activities that coincide with the goals identified above are included in chart 5.2.

Select Adequate Teaching/Learning Resources

Choosing the right teaching/learning resources for youth programs and activities is not always easy. Options are numerous, and budgets often determine what is possible. Vision Quest project leaders across the country said it is helpful to review the array of available resources, and they suggested the following.

Afrocentric resources. Resources that focus attention on the African American experience contribute to youth ministry programs that carry out the goal of cultural awareness and affirmation. These

Chart 5.2. Programs to Achieve Ministry Goals

Youth Ministry Goals	Programs and Activities	
Spiritual Development	• intergenerational worship • teen preaching • teen liturgists • youth choirs • praise café • vacation Bible school • Bible bowls (Bible memorization competitions) • spiritual life retreats and lock-ins • youth evangelism initiatives fostering youth outreach	• congregational worship led by youth (Youth Sundays) • separate youth church • liturgical dance groups • Sunday school • Bible study • Christian values forums • rites of passage • regular youth group meetings
Cultural Awareness and Affirmation	• ethnic programs such as Kwanzaa • Afrocentric praise services • congregational griots (older adult storytellers) • spoken word • mime • rites of passage programs • attendance at drama and other arts events in the community	• black history celebrations • field trips to African American historic sites • Christian rappers • step groups • drummers • youth drama productions • regular youth group meetings

resources include African American Bibles and hymnals, Afrocentric Sunday school materials and information connected with Black History Month, and Afrocentric vacation Bible school materials often available from denominational publishing houses. Additional options include rites of passage resources, such as *Young Lions: Christian Rites of Passage for African American Young Men,*[7] *Daughters of Imani—Planning Guide: Christian Rites of Passage for African American Girls,*[8] *Daughters of Imani—Bible Studies,*[9] and *Orita: Rites of Passage for Youth of African Descent in America.*[10] Consider as well other Afrocentric resources that guide black youths' spiritual development, such as *The Real Deal: A Spiritual Guide for Black Teen Girls*[11] and *Playbook for Christian Manhood: 12 Key Plays for Black Teen Boys,*[12] and African American literature, videos, tapes and other media that highlight experiences of people of African descent. Be proactive in searching the web and

Chart 5.2. Programs to Achieve Ministry Goals (continued)

Youth Ministry Goals	Programs and Activities	
Social Learning	• community service • church-related volunteering • sports activities and teams • teen mentoring of younger youth and children • cross-cultural mixers and study • regular youth group meetings	• mission trips • international aid projects • mentoring by adults • cross-denominational/interreligious mixers and study • youth group open house and block parties
Environmental and Political Awareness and Response	• youth storytelling sessions • community and political action awareness forums • environmental awareness and justice forums	• local and global current events reports and trivia games • responses to racial profiling sessions • regular youth group meetings
Cognitive Development and Educational Preparedness	• teen tutoring • literacy and job training sessions • school achievement celebrations	• study halls • college tours • life skills programs
Emotional Well-Being	• rites of passage programs • forums and workshops on peer pressure, bullying, male and female relationships, date and other violence, and substance abuse	• gender-specific programs focused on black identity and self-esteem • access to counseling and pastoral care
Physical Development	• recreation activities • health and physical fitness programs and camps	• sports teams • health fairs • forums on sex and sexuality

bookstores for newly published resources. Get recommendations from friends and colleagues. Don't be afraid to create your own materials; and include the youth in this creative endeavor. For example, youth in a congregation in the Vision Quest study created an oral history book, *Stories of Our Grandparents*, that was filled with essays they wrote based on their interviews with the oldest members of the congregation. The youth also read the essays during a Sunday worship focused on honoring the oldest members.

Other resources. Uses of a variety of other resources help leaders to carry out youth ministry goals, including a wide range of books, newspapers, magazines, worksheets, maps, talent and spiritual gifts inventories, videos, plays, music, testimonies, photographs, puppets, and speakers. Leaders add that there should be no opposition to drawing on MTV, BET, the Word Network, TBN, and news documentaries.

Be Creative in Putting Programs into Action

Vital youth ministry takes place when leaders involve youth in experiences that engage their thinking and feeling selves. Youth want to be invited to analyze problems, give their opinions, and arrive at solutions. Excellent hope-centered approaches require the teaching expertise and wisdom of the leader, but these approaches also draw on and encourage the input of youth. The leader makes room for what they think about a given topic or activity and how they suggest things might be done. In the words of one leader, "It is taking what we want to happen and teach out of a box, refusing to dumb things down, and freeing ourselves and our youth up to 'go to town' with all that is there for youth to learn and grow. That includes us too." There is also the sense, from that leader's perspective, that "teaching is a reciprocal kind of thing. Really, when you work with young people, you want to create an environment where youth can connect. You have to be ready for how they connect. I'm always amazed to discover that you never know what you're gonna hear, and how they're gonna respond. One time, you'll have everything planned and it goes perfectly. They buy it. Another time, you just end up saying, 'God, have your way!' So you pray that the real teacher shows up and that you're flexible enough to roll with the agenda."

The use of the term "leadership imagination" is an important way to describe the leader's personal statement. In one sense, the formation of leadership imagination happens as leaders understand who youth are and how they become engaged in their own formation. But leadership formation is also about continuing to see through new eyes the youth we lead. It is about developing and using an imaginative capacity of seeing in our mind's eye where our youth are in a particular session or activity and to be open to engage them based on what we see.[13] It extends to asking youth, "What are you thinking? Where are you with this? What would you suggest?" This goes to the heart of hearing our youth.

Can You Hear Me Now? Are You Really Listening?

During a best practices panel discussion led by youth ministry leaders, one of the presenters explained, "In my ministry, the youth have taught me something very important. I think I already knew it, but they brought it home to me. I have learned or relearned that our youth have a voice and they want us to hear them. Sometimes we may get stuck on language and not on content. If we can hear what they have to say, they can not only teach us, but they can also inform us on what it is that they need in this present age. I also have a lot of elderly members in my church. We praise God for that and know they have a voice. But in this twenty-first century, our youth bring new ideas and want new ways of doing things. They can help us with what is needed in this age, if we only listen. My youth teach me a lot."

Actually hearing youth means much more than having a simple conversation and allowing what is said to merely enter our ears. Hearing must actually move to real listening to youth, which is genuinely receiving, making meaning, and responding to what they say.[14] It means learning and becoming well versed in youths' methods of communication and their nonverbal cues, as well as understanding the need for them to experience face-to-face connections in an age of technological connectedness. It was stated earlier that youth develop language patterns that are unique to them. Youth don't expect or necessarily want adults to master or mimic their speech. But, to understand our youth and engage in open and sincere communication, it is important for youth ministry leaders and other adults to have some awareness of the prevailing and often unfolding teen slang, hip hop speech, instant messaging terms, and the latest ebonics (the unique African American dialect that blends black speech with phonics). One youth leader in the Vision Quest

Study said, "If I want to know what the youth are saying and what it means, I just ask them. We have this kind of relationship where I can be the student and they can be the teacher." However, this leader went on to say that "my youth and I have a conversation about what language is best to use in their presentations and leadership in worship or other programs where all ages/stages are present. They are the ones who say that they will use a language everyone will understand, although sometimes a teen word or two will come out. And that's O.K." The point here is that building and maintaining hope-centered relationships with youth entails taking seriously communication with them. In doing so, we show the kind of genuineness, sincerity, and empathy that was highlighted in chapter 2. Of course, we have to work at it!

As mentioned earlier, youth belong to a "gated community" protected by a secret code that restricts the entrance of anyone perceived to be invaders of their space. But there is good news! Evidence shows that effective youth ministries are able to cultivate spaces where youth let leaders into their lives, concerns, thoughts, and fears. Gaining access to this exclusive community, however, requires being available and open to what they have to say to us. Simply put, building listening relationships with youth is the best way to gain access to their world. And we have a perfect role model for doing this. Jesus was a relationship-building expert! He was available to others. He approached others, and then he listened. The Gospels are full of examples of Jesus' radical hospitality shown in his hearing relationship with his twelve disciples and in his conversations with Nicodemus (John 3:1-21), Zacchaeus (Luke 19:1-10), and the woman at the well (John 4:5-42). He listened to people who were disenfranchised, devalued, and ignored by society. If we follow in Jesus' footsteps, we also establish hearing relationships with youth that are nonjudgmental, nonthreatening, welcoming, and nurturing. Consider the following ten tips for listening:[15]

- Make eye contact.

- Create time to be present. Don't hurry.

- Sit or stand close to the youth.

- Lean forward and show a relaxed posture.

- Consider your facial expressions.

- Be careful of interruptions that cut off the youths' train of thought.

- Be sensitive and wait for times to ask questions for clarification.

- Avoid complete silence. Show attentiveness with responses such as "mmmmm," "I hear you," or laughing appropriately.

- Invite additional comments. "Would you like to say more?"

- Show appreciation. "I see." "I understand." "I appreciate what you said." "Thank you."

When leaders and congregations give youth voice and receive what they have to say, we open the way for them to move beyond what often is their feeling of being a stranger rather than being part of the church family. When we have really listened, we prompt their saying what appears in Matthew 25:35, "I was a stranger and you welcomed me." In our listening, we practice *radical hospitality*. Through this demonstration of hospitality, we show a desire to seek out, invite, welcome, receive, care for, and appreciate youth so that they find a spiritual home and discover for themselves the unending richness of life in Christ. "*Radical*" describes that which is drastically different from what often happens. It means going the extra mile.[16]

Youth ministry leaders and other adults can succeed in moving beyond hearing to listening if we endeavor to listen. This means bridging intergenerational miscommunication and building needed trust for youth to open up and for us to allow ourselves to be vulnerable and trust youth as partners in our youth ministry. Furthermore, we are charged to remember the enduring truth that "it's not what you say but how you say it." Recalling this adage will go a long way in listening to what youth have to say. And we must always remember that adults can learn from youth. Effective youth ministry does not occur in a vacuum. We cannot do it alone, and God never intended for us to do it alone. Adults and youth must build community one relationship at a time.

✓CHECK IT OUT

Name three ways you practiced welcoming the community's youth this past year. How was "listening to them" part of the process? What tools that foster a village model do you have in place to reach out to parents and other relatives? Identify some of the best practices within your ministry to welcome youth and adults. How may they be enhanced based on what you have learned from this chapter?

Continuing Our Welcome

Welcoming spaces that intentionally see, reach, and hear youth can curb the exodus of youth from church and provide needed encouragement to youth on their journey toward becoming the persons God has called them to be! Consider the following welcoming strategies.

Recommendations for Cultivating Welcoming Spaces

Seeing. Plan a youth ministry block party. Invite the community in an effort to see those who would not typically come to a church-sponsored, church-hosted activity.

Hearing. Have the youth plan a semiannual forum in a talk show format. Invite local talent to perform in between the talk show "hot topics." Record the forum so that it can be seen later by the youth and reviewed in adult gatherings.

Reaching. Make yourself available during the week and introduce yourself to school administrators, community program developers, and other community leaders. Find ways to connect at high school sports events, competitions, and similar activities. The key here is to go into youths' communities. Gather ideas and suggestions from adults and youth about ways to attract and retain youth.

Welcoming. Host a dress-down worship service or youth group talent search activity and invite the youth to bring their friends and classmates.

Make time during all of these activities to meet youth and their guests. Be sure to get names, addresses, telephone numbers, and e-mail addresses.

Using Effective Methods of Communication

Church website. Invite youth to create and work with your information technology personnel to create their own web page. Enlist their expertise in the maintenance and updating of the web page.

Constant contact. Create an e-newsletter to keep parents and youth updated about ministry activities. Invite youth to report on their ministries and activities.

Flyers. Be creative in producing flyers, and enlist youth to help create and circulate them.

Brochures. Every ministry should have a brochure that can be used for advertising ministries offered at your church. Also consider developing brochures for college students who are new to the area so they know what is happening at your church and can stay connected.

Postcards. Create a postcard for ministry events that are happening at your church or in your community. These are easy to distribute and can also be used as a welcoming card for visitors in the community.

Calling tree. Create an account for a calling service so that you can make one call to reach the entire youth ministry.

Conference lines. Sign up online with a free teleconferencing site that can be used for meetings, prayer calls, and morning devotionals across the miles.

Jesus Christ welcomed youth unconditionally. He was interested in their pasts, their present earthly situations, and their heavenly futures. His example should be emulated during youth ministry moments. Our plans, processes, and programs must be intentionally geared toward proactively pursuing youth. Some of their very lives may depend on it! This means that youth ministry leaders and their teams must work concertedly to see, hear, and reach youth.

The various stories of hope documented in this chapter illustrate the transformative power of welcoming youth ministries. Radical hospitality will enable adults to bridge the many intergenerational chasms that exist to ultimately cultivate welcoming spaces so full of love, laughter, fellowship, fun, creativity, and hope that youth cannot help but enter!

NOTES

1. Meanings of *Sawubona* and *Sikhona* appear in: "Sawubona—I See You," http://africaknows.com/mu/blog/2010/02/i-see-you/, accessed October 12, 2012; Sharon Harris, Untitled Speech, www.kaustschools.org/uploaded/special_events/Sharon_Harris_grad_speech.pdf, accessed October 12, 2012. This story clearly defines the use and context from which the African ritual originates. Also see: Elias Mpofu, ed., *Counseling People of African Ancestry* (Cambridge, England: Cambridge University Press, 2011), 283.

2. Michael Selleck, *United Methodist Youth Handbook* (Nashville: Discipleship Resources, 1999), 12.

3. Sandra L. Barnes, "Religion and Rap Music: An Analysis of Black Church Usage," *Review of Religious Research* 49, no. 3 (2009): 319–38.

4. Robert Schnase, *Five Practices: Radical Hospitality* (Nashville: Abingdon, 2008), 9.

5. Kenda Creasy Dean and Ron Foster, *The Godbearing Life: The Art of Soul Tending for Youth Ministry* (Nashville: Upper Room, 1998), 25.

6. Uses of relational, material, and ideational resources bear kinship to those set forth by Na'ilah Suad Nasir in *Racialized Identities: Race and Achievement Among African American Youth* (Stanford, CA: Stanford University Press, 2012), 110, 137–39. She draws on her research on strategies and resources that foster learning that leads to positive identity formation of African American youth. She highlights the importance of material resources, called physical artifacts, such as desks, backpacks, pencils, and equipment; relational resources such as interpersonal connections; and ideational resources or ideas about the self and what is valued that makes possible one's seeing one's own competence and its outcome.

7. Chris McNair, *Young Lions: Christian Rites of Passage for African American Young Men* (Nashville: Abingdon, 2001).

8. Richelle White, *Daughters of Imani—Planning Guide: Christian Rites of Passage for African American Girls* (Nashville: Abingdon, 2005).

9. Richelle White and Tamara Lewis, *Daughters of Imani—Bible Studies* (Nashville: Abingdon, 2005).

10. Marilyn Mayes and Warren L. Mayes, *Orita: Rites of Passage for Youth of African Descent in America* (Bronx, NY: Faith Works, 2000).

11. Billie Montgomery Cook, *The Real Deal: A Spiritual Guide for Black Teen Girls* (Valley Forge: Judson, 2004).

12. James C. Perkins, *Playbook for Christian Manhood: 12 Key Plays for Black Teen Boys* (Valley Forge, PA: Judson, 2008).

13. The view here of "leadership imagination" draws on Craig Dykstra's and Charles Foster's description of "pastoral imagination" as "a kind of 'internal gyroscope and a distinctive kind of intelligence' and 'a way of seeing into and interpreting the world' that 'shapes everything a pastor thinks and does.'" See Charles R. Foster et al., *Educating Clergy: Teaching Practices and Pastoral Imagination* (San Francisco: Jossey-Bass, 2006), 22. Foster makes reference to Craig Dykstra, "The Pastoral Imagination," *Initiatives in Religion 9*, no. 1 (2001): 2–3, 15.

14. The International Listening Association (ILA) highlights the difference between hearing and listening and emphasizes that listening is more than the physical act of hearing, which we have no control over. Rather, "listening is the active process of receiving, constructing meaning from, and responding to spoken and/or nonverbal messages." See www.listen.org.

15. These tips are drawn from the section entitled "What Is Listening?" in the document, Listening and Critical Thinking, http://highered.mcgraw-hill.com/sites/dl/free/0073385018/537865/pearson3_sample_ch05.pdf, accessed October 14, 2012.

16. See Robert Schnase, "Five Practices: Radical Hospitality," http://fivepractices.org/radical-hospitality/, accessed October 12, 2012.

6
TECH CONNECTIONS
Youth Ministry in a High-Tech World

*Know that wisdom is such to your soul; if you will find it,
you will find a future, and your hope will not be cut off.*
—Proverbs 24:14

In the not-too-far-flung past, it would have seemed incredible to think that we could sit in front of a desktop computer, send and receive an e-mail message, make a call on a cell phone, graduate to a smart phone and tablet, and insist that we could not survive without texting. Now we connect on Facebook, become a blogger, tweet a stranger on the other side of the world, and stream a church service in the comfort of home. Now, it is hard to imagine that much of what has become usual forms of communication are being replaced by still newer means of making connections. But, for today's youth, the present and ever-changing world of media is neither new nor foreign. Our youth are quite comfortable in this world! Depending on our age and stage, adults are either in it or getting used to it. Our churches are slowly beginning to see its possibilities.[1]

In the prologue, we became privy to two youth ministry leaders' straight talk about teens and technology. Mary said, "In too many cases, and in mine, what's happening with the youth just isn't the way I remember growing up. . . . We have . . . a tech-centered generation. . . . It's not all bad—we see the promise. . . . I also have a concern for the church. I hope something new will happen for the sake of our youth. I'm hoping for a different way, a good way forward." Don added, "We don't . . . understand their jargon. . . . The truth is that texting or tweeting is new to some of us. . . . If there's any hope, we've got to deal with the problem of being out of touch with that culture. It ain't about being cool or hip. It's about being relevant."

The world we live in today is vastly different from the one we grew up in! As we can see in Figure 6.1, we live in a high-tech world our youth were born into.

If we are to connect with today's youth, we must be ready to make high-tech connections. But how do we do it? What uses do these connections have for hope-centered youth ministry leadership

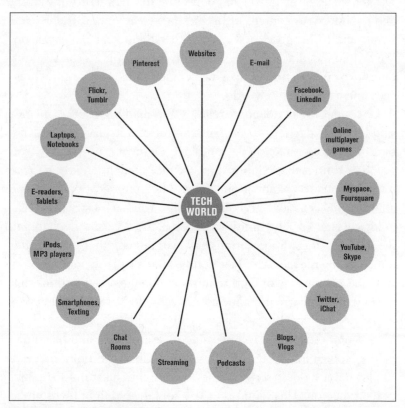

Figure 6.1. Today's tech world.

and youth ministry? Are there churches that are using technology well? What resources are available to help us? What cautions do we need to know about? Let's explore the answers to the questions.

The Truth of the Matter

Let's start with the pivotal belief that even though our high-tech communications are new, the role and necessity of connecting with others is ages old. In fact, the primary message of the gospel handed down to us in the Bible is to go into all the world to make disciples of Jesus Christ (Matthew 28:19-20). Also consider the relevant viewpoint shared on a social media for churches website that Jesus was, in fact, a monumentally successful social networker. As networker, he used the power of connecting through word of mouth; and the infectious content of his message went viral as friends and family shared his good news with others who kept passing it on. We are reminded, too, of the story in Luke 10 of Jesus sending folk out two by two to spread the word of God's life-transforming presence and activity in the world.[2]

Of course, today, adequate relationship-tending practices are not simply confined to face-to-face relationships. Adequacy depends on our use of multi-directional technology. Doing it is not so easy, you say? The truth is that relationships are mediated differently, and we must be open to changing our habits of communication with one another.[3] In her essay, "To Follow Christ: Youth Ministry in a Technological Age," Claire Smith emphasizes the necessity of changing the medium of communication, however difficult that may be, but not changing the message. Her point is that a call to youth ministry grounded in the love of God requires making real connections that are in step with current realities. And technology is surely a big part of today's realities. But, in this tech age, youth ministry must keep as its center the faithful followership of Jesus Christ and be guided by the Holy Spirit. Nothing less will do![4] Charles Fromm makes a similar point in his assertion that our churches must not lose sight of their mission. This requires us to avoid the pitfall of focusing on the "what" of technology instead of on the "Who" of worship.[5]

Making tech connections requires wise choices—choices about what to use, where to use it, and how much to use, whether it is in church worship, church outreach, or youth group activities. Responses from youth ministry leaders in the Vision Quest study tell us that much is yet to be done in making tech connections with youth. Unfortunately, youth ministry leaders are not always tech savvy. As one leader put it, "We can't do what we don't know how to do." In what follows, some examples will be given from leaders on the kinds of connections they've made. We will also explore where to get help.

Connecting in Church

Today techno-based relationship tending is needed and must happen in both face-to-face and distant situations. The congregation's primary gathering place has traditionally been the face-to-face experience in worship. But reaching our youth and others in worship is enhanced by adding techno-media to get across the age-old message of faith. For a moment, sit in on a worship service at Impact Church in Atlanta, Georgia, where connections are made through onsite tech communications using tablets or smartphones and tweeting, and through off-site connections by video streaming.

As we move into the sanctuary and toward our theater-style seats, we become aware of the transformation of the space from its purpose as a school auditorium during the week. We are reminded that we are in church as our eyes become set on the cross in the front. Two large screens are positioned on the left and right stage areas, and recorded gospel music plays as the screens light up through rear projection with moving bands of color and messages of welcome. At the end of the pastor's welcome, the screens become filled with the video of a live presenter, at times a youth, who connects by eye contact, draws our attention to upcoming community events, and extends an invitation to the congregation to respond.

We stand as the screen background changes and the praise team with live band back-up enters and positions themselves in front of microphones. They skillfully lead the whole congregation in singing soul-stirring, spirit-moving songs appearing on the screen. We see the Christian message, hear it as we sing it, and feel the connection to God. Our connection to persons around us and throughout the room becomes real in our unity of bodily response. We later join the community in reading the Scriptures we see on the screens and ready ourselves to receive the sermon. The sermon outline on the screens captures our attention and keeps us focused in addition to the pastor's uses of lesson objects to dramatize, or "drive home," pivotal points. Whether in an intergenerational congregation such as this one or in a youth church where young people are in charge, this kind of connection through technology "speaks" to youth and reaches others as well.

The uses of technologies such as recorded music and large screens for projection of videos, song lyrics, Scripture, sermon outlines, and other video and PowerPoint images during worship are not everywhere, but they are increasing, especially in large churches. Where use of extensive and large equipment is not possible, churches use small screens, laptops and LCD projectors, and flat walls to project selected images, Scripture, and song lyrics. Where this equipment is not available, some churches still attempt to "technologize" worship in a variety of ways, including:

- prerecorded music to accompany liturgical dance, mime, stepping, and dramatization of Scripture called "the Word made flesh";
- prerecorded dramatic readings of Scripture; and
- microphone amplification of praise team and choir music.

The decision to step forward toward technologized worship may take you in the following direction:

- Make your sanctuary a Wi-Fi hotspot for the purposes of giving worshipers access to an electronic copy of the bulletin or other information. Be sure to get someone who can gauge the compatibility of the church structure with a wireless router and who can provide informed cost estimates needed for decision-making and budget-planning.
- Suggest that worshipers use tablets and smartphones to take digital notes and access Scripture using Bible apps.

- Encourage worshipers to tweet about their worship experience and relationship with God as well as raise questions for the pastor to answer later.

What do we need to consider in our uses of technology in worship? Uses of technology in worship should not be entered into lightly. Congregational tech-centered conversations that include youth followed by worship and/or other committee deliberations are helpful means of deciding what is best to do and how best to do it. Take time personally and invite the congregation and youth to critically reflect on the following:

- *Your understanding of worship.* How may technology add to or detract from worship of God and forming and deepening faith? How may it result in glorifying technology rather than God?

- *Your motives.* When considering or using technology in worship, is your only reason to appeal to or satisfy youth? Is your rationale to be up to date or to keep up with the trends? Is it to provide a substitute for printed materials? Is it to add a creative dimension to worship? Is it to enhance everyone's religious experience and understanding of the Christian walk?

- *Your cultural views.* Does your use of technology overly appeal to what you see with your eyes at the expense of hearing with your ears and learning to listen and tell stories to one another like your black ancestors did? Will your focus on the visuals in technology keep you from hearing and remembering songs and Scriptures and imaging "pictures" inside your heads and hearts? Or is it possible to balance seeing and hearing? How?

✓CHECK IT OUT

Take some time now alone or in conversation with a colleague or group to reflect on the following: What kinds of technology, if any, are being used in worship in your congregation? What story would you tell about the decision to engage technology in worship or about why technology is not being used in worship in your congregation? What impact has the use of technology in worship had on youth? Or, if you do not use technology, what impact would you think it might have on youth in or beyond your church?

Connecting beyond Church

In an effort to reach and teach youth beyond the walls of the church, youth ministry leaders and congregations are turning to a wide range of tech tools, from websites containing youth ministry–specific written information and still photography to Facebook contacts and groups, YouTube, Flickr, Vimeo, Twitter, blogs, streaming, podcasts, and webinars. Typically, youth ministry leaders in the Vision Quest study reported and gave tips for using websites employing written content and visual content, mainly still photography. Their point is that we should be sure youth are included in our church websites, making sure that photo and content releases are obtained from parents. Target youth with written content such as the following:

- descriptions of youth ministries
- schedules of youth activities
- location of youth activities
- types of youth activities
- identification of youth ministry leadership
- links to newsletters containing the above
- calendar of activities

Give attention to youth by using visual content such as:

- pictures of youth
- pictures of youth activities in worship, youth meetings, and youth events in the community
- pictures of youth ministry leaders

Because tech in youth culture is highly interactive, be sure to create opportunities for feedback, response, and their input on the content. Organize a youth technology team and make them part of the congregation's tech committee.

The Tech Road Ahead

Black congregations' use of the full range of technologies is still in progress. The earlier mentioned Impact Church in Atlanta, Georgia, and West Angeles Church of God in Christ have exemplary models of ways to engage technology to reach and teach youth. On these church's websites—www.impactdcd.org and www.westa .org—you can find links to parent and youth engagement, uses of Vimeo that make possible video clips, and opportunities to share ideas. You will also find a host of social networking opportunities through Facebook with tabs for sign-up and sign-in; Twitter; slide shows of events and talent; announcements for youth; posts of sermons with sermon synopsis, video and audio presentations, and notes; and a prayer wall. A link to resources and webinars on social media reach out to other churches and nonprofits. Another church, Berean Baptist Church in Brooklyn, New York, gives a creative and helpful example of a youth-centered website at www.bereanbaptist.org. The site features video clips of their youth leadership in worship and in meetings and presentations on the street by their youth group called Drumline.

Taking the next tech step is often hard, but help is available. When we see what is possible, we may easily get excited and want to get involved in technology. But for some leaders, new technologies seem overwhelming, so they pass by opportunities to try them out. Knowing and keeping up with youths' jargon complicates matters further, and then there's the issue of finding help from someone who knows how to use technology.

So, where may help be found? The Resource Corner on page 141 includes informative materials that tell what to do and how to do it, as well as pros and cons on uses of technology in churches that can be applied to ministry with youth.

Will our teens connect with us? If we put forth our best effort to make the tech connection with our youth, how may we be sure they will connect with what we offer? A key way of making the two-way connection happen is to *get the youth involved*. Consulting youth for ideas for content, images, and links will draw their attention and get them plugged in. This approach also helps to fill what leaders in the field of digital media and learning call a "participation gap." It assures preparation of youth to participate fully in the world of tomorrow.[6] In one church, a project was given to the youth to create a youth website that would be linked to the church's website. Go a step further and invite youth to be part of the congregation's tech conversations or committees.

Just because youth appear to be tech savvy, we cannot assume that all of them will have the know-how to navigate well the tech connections we put in place. After deciding on and implementing media that are designed to bring about a working relational connection with youth, bring them together for a CDIWY (Couldn't Do It Without You) session to introduce the media and guide them through the connection processes. You may want to select youth to learn how to use and operate tech equipment. A youth in one of the churches in the Vision Quest study was tapped to operate the video camera from the tripod set up on the sanctuary floor. This youth was also responsible for assuring that the mikes were ready with batteries and positioned correctly for Sunday worship and that the sound levels were properly handled. In multiple ways, we can go far in overcoming the consistent phrases of youth, "Nobody listens to us! Nobody asks us to do anything!"

We need not simply to listen to our youth, but we must become aware of their overall uses of technology. Black teens spend a lot of time on social media. In fact, our teens are ahead of other youth in time spent using mobile devices to talk, send or receive text or e-mail messages and photos or videos, and surf the Web; and tapping into entertainment media, such as watching TV, gaming, and listening to music.[7] Nevertheless, many black youth don't have computers, laptops, or notebooks, not because they don't want them, but because they can't afford them. Others are not in locations where wired or wireless computer installation and home networking are

THE RESOURCE CORNER

Consult helpful resources such as the following and add to the list as you find new ones.

Clifford, Paul A. *Podcasting Church: 21st Century Webcasting for a Timeless Message.* Create Space Independent Publishing Platform, 2011.

Courliss, Jeremy and Hintz, G.P. *Facebook Jesus: Using Facebook to Build and Grow a Church.* Amazon Digital Services, Inc., 2013.

Crawford, Terrace. *Going Social: A Practical Guide on Social Media for Church Leaders.* Kansas City, MO: Beacon Hill Press, 2012.

Fromm, Charles E. Editor. *New Media Technologies in the Service of Worship: 12 Essentials to Engaging With God Through Technology.* San Juan Capistrano, CA: Worship Leader Partnership, 2011.

Hutchinson, Louis J., III. *Restore Together: Urban Ministry in the Context of Technology and Energy in the 21st Century.* Create Space Independent Publishing Platform, 2012.

Kendall, Peggy. *Rewired: Youth Ministry in an Age of IM and MySpace.* Valley Forge, PA: Judson Press, 2007.

Schraeder, Tim and Hendricks, Kevin D. Editors. *Outspoken: Conversations on Church Communication.* Los Angeles: Center for Church Communication, 2011.

Turkle, Sherry. *Alone Together: Why We Expect More from Technology and Less from Each Other.* New York: Basic Books, 2011.

Vogt, Brandon. *The Church and New Media: Blogging Converts, Online Activists, and Bishops Who Tweet.* Huntington, IN: Our Sunday Visitor, 2011.

Wilson, Len and Morre, Jason. "Congregations Liven Sunday Worship with New Media: Part 1." UMC.org, a ministry of United Methodist Communications. www.umc.org/site/c.1wL4KnN1LtH/b.../Media...Worship/.../link.asp

present. So, for our youth, the digital divide still exists and they connect through mobile media.[8]

A key way to connect with teens is through Facebook, but be sure to talk with them about using it with safety and respect. Youth ministry leaders in the Vision Quest study told of sessions with youth on "TechTalk" that emphasize how what is placed on the Internet becomes information for the whole world. These sessions hit hard at the potential negative impact of posting provocative photos, uncomplimentary language, gossip, and forms of bullying. They are means of helping youth grasp meanings of i-hospitality. Here are some ideas for connecting on Facebook:

- Create a Facebook youth group. A helpful online resource is "How to Create a New Facebook Group" found on www.wiki how.com/create-a-new-Facebook-Group.

- Make a date for youth to post favorite Scriptures and send messages of inspiration and encouragement to friends.

- Remind youth to check out the church's website for announcements and other targeted information of interest to youth.

- Invite youth to share their prayer requests and praise reports and songs that inspire.

- Post youth's thoughts on topics explored in youth group meetings and youths' creative writing, including mini-sermons, spoken word, or raps.

- Invite posts of pictures of community service or other inspiring youth activities.

Text Talk. Texting with teens ushers us into a whole new language world. Youth use a kind of shorthand that speeds up texting, and adults have picked up on it too. Who among us has not received a text that included lol (laughing out loud), thx (Thanks), omg (Oh my God), U2 (You too), wbs (Write back soon), or swak (Sealed with a kiss)? Youth ministry leaders do not need to talk like teens any more than we are called to dress like them. However, in our tech connections with them, we can agree to use the same shortcuts. In some youth groups, leaders engage youth in critical dialogue on language codes that respect and codes that harm others. Their intent is to emphasize that there is an ethical dimension to participating in social media and a moral responsibility that Christians accept for themselves. In this conversation, youth leaders also invite youth to create and publish Christian codes for use in texting.

The message is clear: in various forms, social media extend the social spaces we live in. They provide new opportunities for youth ministry leaders, youth, and others in our church "villages" to relate and learn together. For this to happen, however, we must bring youth on board with the decisions we make and lead them in what to do with technology. (See Peggy Kendall's book, *Rewired: Youth Ministry in an Age of IM and MySpace*, Judson Press, 2007, for more creative ideas and practical cautions about integrating social media and technology in ministry with youth.)

There's a Bigger Picture Out There

We are in the midst of a technology revolution. More and more media are being created every day. They are extensions of ourselves—our identities—and the world we live in. We have the tech devices. We use them. Our youth have them. They use them. These tech means of connecting with one another are here to stay. So what we do with them for the sake of our youth matters! It is no secret that because of commercial media outside the church, young people today access all sorts of information and images, gain new knowledge, and refine what they already know. They connect with friends, meet new people, and expand their understanding of others different from themselves and their culture.

But on the negative side, our youth also come into contact with high incidences of violence, bullying, other kinds of aggression, and other forms of behavior and attitudes that have the power to shape their views of life and choices about how to live.[9] We are right to raise concern about whether violence in our communities is somehow related to what our youth see in media. Concern has also moved to "outcries over rising levels of aggression, obesity, substance abuse, eating disorders and unsafe sexual behavior among youth" because of commercial media.[10] What is happening affects Christian youth in our churches, and it spills over to unchurched youth we must reach out to. What can we do?

Don't hesitate to engage youth in talk about the good, the bad, and the ugly. Everything about media is not positive. There are realities of the good, the bad, and the ugly in the world beyond the church that ministry with youth must address. The point here is that as youth ministry leaders, we are afforded a great opportunity and are given great responsibility for engaging our youth in tough conversations about the content of media that is accessed in the world we live in and the impact it can have on their character. We are on the front lines of helping youth judge what they see, understand, and do, resulting from watching TV, surfing the web, participating in social media, playing video games, and listening to music. Consider doing the following:

- Create an opportunity for youth to share about a recently viewed movie, a video game they played, Facebook content, or music they have listened to and tell what went into their choosing that entertainment.

- Select one or two of the youths' choices and ask them to describe the content, the language, and the message that were communicated.

- Invite the group to decide on what was positive and/or negative in the content, the language, and the message.

- Engage the whole group in discussing what might happen if the content, language, and message were played out in relationships with them and others they know. Ask them to highlight the actions that would take place, the feelings they and others would have, and what might be the outcome.

- Create small groups to develop a multimedia presentation on the outcome in real life in light of Romans 13:8-10. This kind of presentation calls them to decide how they may incorporate technology in hope-centered ways (e.g., visuals from the web, music from the computer, teen-made PowerPoints, or posters with graphics).[11]

- Form a panel of youth to be judges who share what constitutes helpful and harmful content in TV movies, videos, video games, social networking, and music.

- Have the whole group brainstorm how the judgments may be used to influence their choices of media.

The reality of face-to-face connections versus techno-connections. Youths' connection with media culture has a way of disrupting or reducing opportunities for face-to-face relationships. Youth ministry leaders tell of youth in a youth group meeting who text another youth sitting next to them. In addition, youth tell of their family members texting one another while all are at home. Some fear that youth are losing the ability to relate face-to-face and that the communication gap is widening between youth and adults. There is no substitute for being fully present in the flesh to others. We can disappear online, but in our homes, schools, churches, and communities, we can't hide. How we treat one another in the flesh and in the now cannot be escaped. An important part of our ministry with youth as we move forward into the future of increasing technology may be more intentional efforts to draw their attention and our own to the wisdom of being in up-close relationships. This is wisdom that ensures our hope will not be cut off (Proverbs 24:14). And this wisdom is knowing and acting on the gift that we are to one another, the loving care we must give to one another, and the welcome we owe one another, lest we entertain angels without knowing it (Hebrews 13:1-3).

✓ CHECK IT OUT

Since each ministry setting is unique, each of us has a different vision of what we would like to do with technology, and each faces different trials and triumphs in making techno-connections. Create some time individually, with a colleague, or in a group to tell your triumphs, trials, and vision for

Chart 6.1. Tech Reflection Guide

Triumphs	Trials	The Way Forward
Tell about a successful tech connection with youth in your congregation using technology in worship, such as the following: • screens with projected words and images, and live presentations • recorded music to accompany liturgical dance, mime, stepping, and dramatization of Scripture • recorded dramatic readings of Scripture • microphone amplification of praise team and choir music Tell about a successful tech connection with youth beyond church: • website with youth ministry information • uses of Facebook, YouTube, Flickr, Vimeo, Twitter, blogs, streaming, or webinars • youth helping to make decisions about uses of technology in your church Tell about efforts to learn how youth are using social media: • sessions that engage youth in conversation about movies and videos they are watching, video games they are playing, etc. Tell about resources you have used to help make good tech connections.	Tell about the following: • efforts started to make tech connections with youth in congregational worship that were not completed • efforts that you wished would have been more successful • efforts that failed Tell about the following: • efforts to establish a website containing youth ministry information that you would like to see improved • efforts to add social media but did not have the resources to do it Tell about the following: • your desire to connect with how youth are using social media but haven't had opportunity yet to do it • the need to develop sessions that engage youth in conversation about movies and videos they are watching, video games they are playing, etc. Tell about the following: • difficulties in finding tech support resources • greater efforts needed to involve youth in decision making about uses of technology in your church	• What is your vision for making tech connections with youth in your congregation? • What would you like to see happen in worship? • What techology would be desirable to reach beyond the church (e.g., websites, Facebook, YouTube, Flickr, Vimeo, Twitter, blogs, streaming, webinars)? • In what new or renewed ways might you discover how youth are using social media? • What resoures might you draw upon?

making tech connections with youth in your congregation. Use chart 6.1 as a guide to your reflection. End with a time of prayer for God's guidance in the process forward.

NOTES

1. Thirty-one churches were part of an ethnographic study in the Vision Quest research project. As part of that study, information was collected on the presence and contents of each church's website. Eighteen of the churches had websites. Only nine made reference to youth. Five churches used language in their vision statements that made mention of youth. Churches varied in what they included about youth ministries, from sparse to wide-ranging information. A few included pictures and social networking media.

2. See United Methodist Communications (UMCom), "Social Networking for Churches," www.umcom.org/site.../b.../k.../Social_Media_for_churches. htm, accessed August 10, 2012. The article makes the point that the continuous networking process begun in Jesus' day resulted in 2.18 billion Christians in the world by 2010, or about a third of the global population. In the U.S., eight in ten (78.4%) adults called themselves Christian, according to the 2011 Barna report. However, it is important to add that this figure compares to 86 percent claiming to be Christian in 1990. And, added to the 2011 figures is the declining membership in Protestant churches (51.3% of the overall adult population), compared to between 60 and 65 percent through the 1970s and 1980s, with youth less affiliated than ever before. These data are found in: Pew Forum on Religion & Public Life, "Global Christianity: A Report on the Size and Distribution of the World's Christian Population," December 19, 2011, www.pewforum.org/Christian/Global-Christianity-exec.aspx, accessed April 2, 2013.

3. Charles E. Fromm, ed., "Introduction," *New Media Technologies in the Service of Worship: 12 Essentials to Engaging with God through Technology* (San Juan Capistrano: Worship Leader Partnership, 2011), 1.

4. Claire A. Smith, "To Follow Christ: Youth Ministry in a Technological Age," 1–13, in Peggy Kendall, Claire A. Smith, Tim Keel, Ryan Langeland, and Sondra H. Matthaei, *Youth Ministry in a Technological Age* (2011), 13. Orders through Xlibris Corporation, Orders@Xlibris.com.

5. Charles E. Fromm, ed., "Introduction," *New Media Technologies in the Service of Worship*, 1.

6. Henry Jenkins with Katie Clinton, Ravi Purushotma, Alice J. Robison, and Margaret Weigel, "Confronting the Challenges of Participatory Culture: Media Education for the 21st Century," 3. An occasional paper on digital media and learning, the MacArthur Foundation, 2006, www.digitallearning.macfound.org/atf/cf.../JENKINS_WHITE_PAPER.PDF, accessed April 8, 2012.

7. See Pew Research Center, "Americans and Their Cell Phones," The Center's Internet & American Life Project, April 26–May 22, 2011 Spring Tracking

Survey, http://pewresearch.org/pubs/2083/cell-phones-texting-internet-photos; and Adam C. Williams III, "Spotlight: Dr. S. Craig Watkins Examines Emerging Trends amongst Black Youth with Social and New Media Technologies," Black Media Council, 2, http://blackmediacouncil.wordpress.com/2011/01/20/spotlight-dr-craig-watkins-new-book, accessed April 8, 2012.

8. Josh Karp, "To Be Young, Digital, and Black," Spotlight on Digital Media and Learning, http://spotlight.macfound.org/featured.../to-be-young-digital-and-black, accessed April 8, 2012.

9. Gregory C. Ellison II, "Fantasy as Addition to Reality? An Exploration of Fantasy Aggression and Fantasy Aggrace-ion in Violent Media," Plenary presentation at 2012 Annual Meeting of the Society for Pastoral Theology, Santa Barbara, CA, June 2012. Throughout his paper, Ellison affirms the claim that there is a direct correlation between youths' exposure to violent images in media, music, Internet, and video games and their developing and engaging in violent behaviors. Repeated exposure has the effect of conditioning youth to what they see. Violence becomes normalized for them. The fantasy of what they see blends with the real world.

10. Susan Gigli, "Children, Youth and Media around the World: An Overview of Trends & Issues," Report of the InterMedia Survey Institute for UNICEF, 4th World Summit on Media for Children and Adolescents, Rio de Janeiro, Brazil, April 2004, 4, www.unicef.org/videoaudio/intermedia_revised.pdf, accessed April 8, 2012.

11. A full discussion about the uses of tech media as educational tools appears in: Rosen, Larry D. *Rewired: Understanding the iGeneration and the Way They Learn.* New York: Palgrave Macmillan, 2010.

7
REAL HOPE
Programs of Promise

We always give thanks to God for all of you and
mention you in our prayers, constantly remembering
before our God and Father your work of faith and labor of
love and steadfastness of hope in our Lord Jesus Christ.
—1 Thessalonians 1:2-3

A youth ministry leader met with a Vision Quest interviewer to re-flect on the nature, challenges, and promise of ministry with youth. In a quiet moment of reflection on the question, "What gives you the greatest sense of encouragement and hope?" the leader shared these words with deep feeling and sincerity:

> In the middle of all the challenges of youth ministry, all of the concerns the youth bring, all of the things we need to get the ministry going and keep it up and running, there's always the next step. In that step, we say, "How do we prepare for the lock-in that's coming up Saturday night? Did we tell the organist about the music for the fifth Sunday youth service?" In the middle of it all, there's a rhythm and the beat goes on. And, when it's all said and done, you know what? We've seen the youth come. We've seen them fall in love with the church and God. We've had to say at times, "Go home! We've got to lock up!" And, get this, one day, one of the kids said, "I just don't even want to go home!"

Youth leaders are quick to say that much is needed to assure excellent hope-centered ministry with youth in the black church.

We've noted prevailing challenges in previous chapters. We are also aware of results from our national church survey that 15.6 percent of the surveyed black congregations do not sponsor any youth programs, and that this lack of sponsorship was largely due to lack of youth involvement, lack of parental involvement, and lack of church involvement. The challenge remains, and we must not lose sight of it! However, it is also clear that the majority (84.4 percent) of our churches carry out some form of youth ministry. Churches choose programs and activities according to what is considered appropriate for their particular environments and depending on the resources that are available to support them. Churches in the Vision Quest study sponsored sixteen programs. The list of programs is included in table 7.1, along with the percentage of churches using each program on the list. Note that the most popular programs included congregational worship led by youth, community service, programs to counter peer pressure and boost self-esteem, regular youth group meetings, youth choir, and ethnic programs.[1]

What's Happening is Good!

What is happening in today's youth programs of promise comes from the kind of holy boldness mentioned in the beginning of chapter 2. This holy boldness builds on leaders' reliance on the promises of God in Scripture, which instill us with hope. Christ promised never to leave us or forsake us (Hebrews 13:5). Jesus promised to go prepare a place for us (John 14:2-3), send the Holy Spirit to comfort us (John 15:26; 16:7), and to be with us always as we follow the Great Commission (Matthew 28:19-20). And there are many more biblical promises where those came from! In like fashion, youth ministry programs of promise strive to create, maintain, and grow experiences that black youth can rely on to meet their spiritual and temporal needs and wants. The very lives of many youth depend on such programs.

Varying numbers of youth ministry programs have resulted from the biblical promise on which leaders and congregations have moved forward. The majority (79.8 percent) of the surveyed

Table 7.1. Types of Youth Programs Sponsored by Black Churches

Program Type	Percentage
Congregational worship led by youth	89.0
Community service	86.5
Peer pressure or self-esteem	85.8
Regular youth group meetings	84.8
Youth choir	83.9
Ethnic programs (Kwanzaa, Black History)	82.8
Art	76.8
Counseling	76.8
Mentoring	71.1
Crime/violence	69.8
Sexuality	64.9
Tutoring, literacy, and job training	51.9
Sports	41.4
Rites of passage	36.7
Gender-specific programs	36.0
Separate youth church	35.8

Vision Quest 2009: N = 703

churches sponsor one to eleven youth programs. A small number of them (3.4 percent) have as many as twelve or more programs.[2]

The truth is that much is happening in black congregations to guide, support, and advance the holistic growth of black youth. Well-planned, spiritually motivating ministries that instill knowledge, life skills—and hope—in black youth are occurring. Yes! Ministries that make us say "Wow" are taking place to the degree that youth fall in love with God and don't want to go home when it's time to turn the lights out and lock up the meeting room. Youth are involved in numerous and creative ways, and in many cases, congregations and communities both support and receive benefits from youth ministry efforts.

Interestingly, many often assume that large churches in metropolitan areas are alone in their ability to offer multiple or effective programs with, by, and for youth. But leaders in the Vision Quest national study and observations of programs and activities in churches of all sizes and regions affirm that size and place do not necessarily limit a congregation's ability to make youth ministry come alive. It's worth saying again! From what appeared in the study, programs of promise prove that mighty steps are being taken and the beat does indeed go on! The remainder of this chapter is all about showcasing programs of promise. Our primary purpose is to share best practices in youth ministry programs across the country as means of celebrating what is taking place, to give ideas of what is possible, and to inspire further action. The programs and activities described here are testaments to what well-prepared, imaginative youth ministry leaders, dedicated staff, as well as supportive congregations and pastors can do to transform the lives of the youth they serve. We will close with ten power steps for moving forward.

Programs of Promise

Programs of promise connect in significant ways to the key ministry goals mentioned in chapter 5 that respond to characteristics of youth (see page 120). Recall that these goals centered on spiritual development, cultural awareness and affirmation, social learning, environmental and political awareness and response, cognitive development, cognitive development and educational preparedness, emotional well-being, and physical development. All of the programs that exist in churches to address these goals are not necessarily sponsored solely by a congregation. Some congregations partner or have alliances with other organizations, such as Girl Scouts and Boy Scouts, to provide for the youth they serve. Best practices occurring in selected programs of promise are summarized in the following sections, in accordance with the ministry goals set in chapter 5.

Spiritual Development Best Practices

Youth grow spiritually and gain understanding of Christian discipleship through firsthand involvement in worship, community events and practices, and opportunities to lead and serve.

Best Practice 1. A Presbyterian church in an urban California neighborhood with 71 members engages youth in the following ways:

- as liturgists;

- as ushers, either as a group or with adult ushers;

- as teachers, teaching assistants, or helpers in Christian education endeavors; and

- as worship monitors who sit beside younger children to show them what is going on and to maintain appropriate behavior. In this way, worship remains an intergenerational experience.

The pastor said, "The placement of youth in these capacities results from recognition of the gifts of the youth." The pastor, who is also responsible for youth ministry, told of a high school freshman who assists in Christian education by teaching the younger students. He described the young man as "very good at lesson planning and asking the students questions about what they'd been reading to make sure they are all on the same page." Because the youth had shown interest, the pastor asked the Christian education teacher to just "try him out" one day. The pastor added, "And then it was like, 'Whoa! He's really good at this! He's good, very good, and people respect how he runs it.'"

The pastor added, "When we ask people to come to the altar for prayer time, almost every week there's a young person asking for prayer. You can argue about young people that you don't really see active; but when you see them as ushers, when you see them as liturgists, when you see them active in the church, then there is not a whole lot that you can argue about. Besides, it shows that youth are leaders today. We don't have to wait until tomorrow. You know, I think that has changed much of the dynamics of this church. And my hope is to increase their involvement."

Best Practice 2. In a Lutheran church in an urban Michigan area with 300 to 350 members, youth provide leadership every Sunday during worship in the form of a youth praise team, worship leader, and ushers. There is no separate youth church. The church's active youth ministry, which has about 50 young people, meets on the first and third Fridays each month.

Best Practice 3. "To empower youth," said a pastor in a 76-member United Methodist church in a small Alabama town, "the youth are routinely brought into leadership during Sunday worship." The pastor continued, "Sometimes they are in charge of the whole service and all I do is preach, but there have been times that a young person has preached as well. The kids are creative. They asked me if they could do things differently, and I said it's okay. The congregation has received them well."

Best Practice 4. CHG (Club Holy Ghost) is a Saturday night service held by a 1,100-member AME church in Washington, DC. The service was designed to be an alternative worship experience for high school youth and college students, but it also draws community people. The CHG is located in a separate building from the church and has youth trustees and stewards, and the youth are given opportunities to lead in the service, including reading Scripture, ushering, singing, wisdom reading, and dancing. There is no dress code. CHG is a church within a church. CHG leaders reach out to those who attend with greeters who welcome participants as they enter and offer words of gratitude for their attendance as they leave. First-time participants get a "glad you came, please come again" note or a text message. CHG also has a Facebook page and sends invitations to attend via that page. Some other members of the church also come because of their preference for worship on Saturday night. The benefit of this specially named separate worship experience for youth was captured in a youth's words: "If it wasn't for this youth stuff, I wouldn't be at church. If it wasn't for their offering us opportunities where people our age can come together and worship, I wouldn't even come to church."

CHG provides an opportunity for black youth to worship in a space that is created by and for them. They are responsible for the entire service and use technology common to their generation. This specially designed effort, including the informal dress code, meets youth "where they are" and "when they want" using tools that resonate with their experiences. They realize the Holy Ghost can be fully present in a youth-led service just as this presence is felt in adult-led service.

Best Practice 5. BEEF (Being Educated Enough to Flee) is the name given to Wednesday night Bible study in a small Baptist church in Tennessee. The sessions focus on educating youth in the Word of God so that they can "take off running" toward a promising future. The sessions are also to "teach youth self-accountability . . . that they are responsible and in charge of their actions, and that there is no reason why they cannot aspire to be and actually become professionals in a variety of vocations. BEEF is about instilling values."

The creative format is a spiritual response to the question from an old Wendy's television commercial, "Where's the beef?" The youth at this church have found it as they create their own space to study Scripture and learn strategies to live empowered, godly lives. BEEF is also unique in its focus on running forward positively rather than running away from the many negative situations and experiences black youth face. By focusing on self-efficacy and intentional decision making, the weekly encounters create a space where black youth can meet in solidarity with each other and with Christ.

Additional Best Practices. Other examples of youth activities in churches of various sizes include making presentations during vacation Bible school, bringing the Word in Sunday worship, creating and performing dramas and puppet shows, using mime, playing instruments, and running the sound system during worship.

Cultural Awareness and Affirmation Best Practices

Black churches contribute to their youths' seeing themselves as unashamed black persons by engaging youth in activities that honor their blackness and increase their awareness of black history. Youth leaders shared a number of Afrocentric practices, from black history celebrations to rites of passage programs.

Best Practice 1. A 450-member African Methodist Episcopal (AME) church in Michigan conducted two creative Black History Month celebrations. The youth leader described one celebration: "We wanted the youth to learn about black history right in the church from people who have made contributions. We have a lady who is a hundred years old, one lady who is ninety-nine, and a gentleman who is ninety-eight. So the three age groups in the Young People's Division went to visit these people and interviewed them. The youth presented what they learned on the Sunday following their visits. The questions asked included: 'How old were you when you came to Christ? How long have you been a member of this church? When you were my age, what were you doing? What were your hopes and dreams? What goals and dreams have you accomplished in life? What advice would you give to me today?' The youth gained a new appreciation for the older generation. The older people gained a new appreciation for the younger generation because of what they learned about them. It has been beneficial, and the congregation enjoyed it."

The youth leader continued, "On another occasion, we presented a 'Who Is It?' activity in worship that included senior adults in our church and black leaders in our community. We didn't say who the person was, but the young people shared ideas. Then they asked the congregation, 'Who are we talking about?' It's been a great way of understanding that black history happens right in our church and community."

Best Practice 2. A Vision Quest project researcher observed an Afrocentric village praise service in a 2,000-member Baptist church in metropolitan New York City. The special celebration was led by a group of young people wearing kente cloth stoles. They were seated in the front row. The men's choir and men of the church wore similar kente cloth stoles and were seated on one side of the church. The women were dressed in white and seated on the other side of the church. Each youth was asked to stand as her or his name was called. Recognition was given to young people who had received awards and accolades in the community, school, or church; had shown progress on their monthly reports in school; were on the honor roll; or had sports achievements. College students were also acknowledged. The recipients of the church's "Youth of the Year" and "Youth Member of the Week" were asked to speak.

Best Practice 3. Drumline is also an activity of the aforementioned metropolitan New York area Baptist church and is an ongoing endeavor reminiscent of the drumline featured in the 2002 movie *Drumline*, depicting show-style marching bands performing during half-time at football games of historically black colleges and universities. The idea for the activity at the church evolved from the youth ministry leader's role as a section leader of the drumline while he was a marching band scholarship student in college. But the leader also said that the church had a drum and bugle corp in the 1970s and '80s. Begun in 2008 during the youth pastor's seminary field placement year, the new activity included drumming and stepping. It drew mainly unchurched neighborhood school kids who began tapping sticks on tables. There were no drums. The activity continued, and drums were later donated after the youth ministry leader became a full-time staff member.

The leader said that the congregation's ownership of Drumline became real because it was introduced as a whole community participatory experience. "Consequently, one of the first things I did was to write a cadence that was in tribute to the church so the whole congregation sings with the drumline, paying homage to the church's history. . . . It brings them into it. They see themselves as one with this. The drumline represents dialogue. It teaches/allows youth and adults to learn the give-and-take of conversation through the talking of the drums. The youth who participate in Drumline are also learning to trust each other's ability to communicate. Drumline has become a vehicle for wider community building, because we go out into the community a lot and do all the block parties. What has happened is that it has become our main vehicle of outreach. I have seen we have a new energy at our church. The elderly population is excited about what is going on with the youth and support them, which is something we did not have in the beginning. The personalities of the youth have come out."

Best Practice 4. Kupanda Kuelekea Uboro Rites of Passage Program (KKU ROP; Swahili for "rising to excellence") is a five-month program for teens ages twelve to eighteen at an AME church in the Atlanta metro area. The program is a Christian and Afrocentric program designed to help develop youth into well-rounded young adults. It provides opportunities for adolescents to prepare themselves physically, socially, emotionally, intellectually, and culturally for passage to adulthood through topics such as biblical study, African American culture and history, conflict/anger management, financial management, Christian living for teens, and career and college preparation. The program is based on the Nguzo Saba value system of Umoja (unity), Kujichagulia (self-determination), Ujima (collective work and responsibility), Ujamma (collective economics), Nia (purpose), Kuuma (creativity), and Imani (faith).

Social Learning and Emotional Well-Being Best Practices

Black churches in our survey put forth efforts to place youth with adults so they could learn positive ways of relating in the world and serving with and apart from adults in and beyond the church. This effort in youth ministry often included attention to other aspects of ministry. Consequently, the following best practices that focus on social-relational development also consist of practices directed toward other ministry goals.

Best Practice 1. Save Our Sons (SOS) is an outreach program of a 2,500-member Baptist church in a midsize Florida town. Save Our Sons utilizes positive role models to guide young black males in the community toward their becoming mature, productive role models in society. The organization engages youth in values-building activities, athletics, and academic supports. Begun in 2008, the program resulted from the church's desire to address increasing gang activity in the community, to offer an alternative to violence and drugs, and to provide male role models for young men whose fathers were absent or inactive in their lives. The director said, "We are trying to build a connection, fill a gap, and expose these young men to different experiences. We try to uphold them and lift them up. A part of our pedagogy is the use of interactive workshops where the young men put questions in a bucket that the leaders will pull out and answer. This approach gives them an opportunity to ask things anonymously."

Best Practice 2. An African Methodist Episcopal Zion (AMEZ) church in a small Illinois town held a lock-in titled "CTRL/ALT/DELETE" that gave specific attention to demeaning language and images found in hip-hop culture and today's media. Workshop facilitators guided youth in reflecting on two main themes. One was "Alter Your Thinking." In this workshop, teens listened to selected rap music and discussed the impact on their uses of language resulting from the music. They considered answers to questions about what was portrayed about them in the language, how they would like to be seen, and what their image of a Christian is. The second workshop theme was "Control Your Actions." This workshop engaged youth in talking openly about demeaning language they use, why they use it, how it makes them feel when others use it to refer to them, and what they intend to do to "represent" as Christians.

Daily Issues Awareness and Best Practices

Black churches recognize that our youths' everyday stories are filled with challenges they need help addressing. To this end, youth ministries in these churches engage youth in critical reflection, drawing from the Christian faith to turn challenges into opportunities for living with hope.

Best Practice 1. TGIF (Teens Gathered in Faith) is a youth ministry initiative in an 1,800-member AME church in California. The program was named by the youth to appeal to teens within and beyond the church. TGIF focuses youths' attention on their everyday lives and ways of addressing issues they face. Church members provide dinner at their meetings on Fridays from 7:00 to 9:00 p.m. Youth engage in studies, using biblical tools designed to speak to their everyday lives and issues. Once per quarter a representative from a community agency, such as the health department or police department, speaks to the youth on a topic of special interest.

Best Practice 2. A Presbyterian church in Atlanta, Georgia, hosts an annual International Day. On that day youth are engaged in learning about other cultures and demonstrating what they learned in a culminating event that at various times involves wearing clothes that are native to the country they have explored, serving food from designated cultures, presenting culturally diverse music, or sponsoring song-fests using music from different cultures, and a game-fest in which participants play popular and unique games from other cultures.

Best Practice 3. A number of different churches across the country have sponsored:

- bullying prevention events

- conflict management workshops

- gang prevention forums

- combined activities with youth in churches or worship environments of cultures differing from their own and the dominant culture (e.g., African, Puerto Rican, Brazilian, Muslim, inter-cultural churches)

- block parties to welcome new residents in the community and invite their presence in the church.

Cognitive Development and Educational Preparedness Best Practices

Concern for school dropouts and attention to educational preparedness have resulted in black churches paying attention to opportunities that encourage youth to consider their futures and plan courses of action based on the values and norms of the Christian faith. The churches stress the importance of education and vocational preparedness. Many host college tours. Others have college prep days. Still others provide tutoring and study halls and make announcements about times and places for college entrance exams such as the SAT (Scholastic Aptitude Test) and ACT (American College Test).

Best Practice 1. The aforementioned AME church in California partners with a local university and representatives of black colleges in the area for purposes of keeping college education before black youth. A youth conference is held on a specified weekend each year that leads up to Youth Day. On this weekend, the church has local and black college representatives come to provide information on their educational programs and to encourage youth to go to college. They give three- to five-minute presentations during the Sunday morning worship. Then after the morning worship, tables are set up on the lower level of the church, and representatives are on hand to provide information and answer questions.

Best Practice 2. A small Baptist church in a Tennessee town sponsors a graduation gala to celebrate youths' graduation from high school. According to the youth ministry leader, "We know that every graduate may not have a family that celebrates their accomplishments or may not have the money to do it. So we want them to know that here we care, and no matter how, we've got to do it. We want our youth to know that we're going to do it for you!"

Physical Development Best Practices

Black churches take note that teens are in the process of developing in multiple ways, and their physical development is among the most prominent changes that signal their movement toward adulthood. Youth ministry activities respond to these changes by providing activities that promote healthy development and engage youth in conversations about healthy life choices and self-care.

Best Practice 1. Young Men of Valor and Young Women of Valor is a mentoring program of a 1,000-member Church of God in Christ in Los Angeles, California. The program focuses on health, hygiene, and etiquette using biblical tools. The program also sponsors social activities focused on entertainment and relationship building. Program outreach extends to local high schools in close proximity to the church. This outreach includes inviting high school faculty, students, and athletic teams to participate in church-hosted pizza parties. Participants receive an invitation to attend the church's Sunday morning teen church.

Best Practice 2. Men of Faith is a program for males sponsored by a 200-member United Methodist church in Los Angeles, California. The program activities consist of mentoring by men in the church that takes place every first and third Saturday in addition to periodic field trips. A key part of the program is the young men's enrollment in a basketball league that plays games on Saturdays.

Additional Best Practices

Ministry leaders have proudly cited many other, less traditional programs and activities designed to bring Christianity alive in the hearts, minds, and souls of youth. In fact, about 86 percent of the youth leaders in a smaller part of the Vision Quest study mentioned specific youth programs or activities of which they are particularly proud, including the following:

- dance ministry (AME church in Bermuda)

- youth choir and liturgical dance team (AME church in Georgia)

- puppet ministry (Baptist church in Ohio)

- Signs of Praise mime ministry (AME church in Georgia)

- step team (COGIC church in Virginia)

Youth also like to name their youth groups and activities in ways that go beyond the functional and traditional church or denominational names. The earlier mentioned CHG (Club Holy Ghost), TGIF (Teens Gathered in Faith), and BEEF (Being Educated Enough to Flee) are examples. Creative naming practices appeal to youth and increase participation. These practices along with all that have already been described confirm the presence of excellent hope-centered youth ministry taking place in black churches.

Each of the above programs illustrates some of the imaginative ways youth ministry leaders engage youth. From rites of passage to music, dance, puppetry, singing, stepping—all of these approaches reflect contemporary efforts to attract and retain black youth. And they work! Increasing numbers of black churches are realizing they must think outside the box if they wish to capture the attention, hearts, and minds of youth.

The Case for Black Ethnic Programs

African Americans have made great strides economically, politically, and socially in the United States. However, the reality of inequality, discrimination, prejudices, and stereotypes based on race (as well as class, gender, and sexual orientation), along with the legacy of slavery continues to impact the lives of most black people. Some people believe that the election of the first black U.S. president signaled the end of racism. But research by scholars such as Cornel West, Joe Feagin, and Eduardo Bonilla-Silva[3] show that racism is alive and well. It is imperative that black youth learn about their singular heritage and history, the strengths found in the black community, and the challenges yet to be met. Moreover, they must be taught how to successfully negotiate society to maximize their experiences and hopefully minimize trauma, disillusionment, and sadness. But learning about black history is more than being prepared to counter negativity—it's about being empowered as youth learn about and experience the many wonderful, exciting ways that black people have influenced society and the world.

Churches that center on black ethnic programs and activities today follow a long history of churches that have offered programs, teaching, and preaching, and have provided living models to instill racial pride. Imaginative youth ministry must instill hope in black youth in several ways. First, the fortitude exhibited by blacks during slavery and their impressive post-slavery accomplishments should provide black youth with a strong sense of hope. Additionally, ministries should prepare black youth for spiritual and secular forms of success, confidence, self-efficacy, historical knowledge, unconditional racial love, and personal racial pride that will gird them up if they should encounter racial oppression. The well-known statement "Say it loud—I'm black and I'm proud!" must be part of the mantra of programs of promise. Below are comments from youth ministry leaders who rely on Afrocentric resources:

- "Remarkable educational outcomes have resulted from church members sharing personal stories of their involvement in the Civil Rights Movement, posting pictures of black heroes and sheroes in the educational building hallways, telling our church's history." (AME church in Georgia)

- "We use Urban Ministries Sunday school materials, videos, music, pictures, and worksheets." (AME church in Georgia)

- "We use curricula designed by our director of Christian Education and Center for African Biblical Studies, videos, etc." (Presbyterian church in Georgia)

- "Our publishing house provides materials that are Afrocentric. We use all of them." (AME church in Georgia)

- "All of our study materials are Afrocentric." (Baptist church in Alabama)

Urban Ministries (UMI) is the specific resource cited most often. Leaders also said that special attention is paid to Afrocentric issues during Black History Month and during their church denominational celebrations.

Sadly, some black people incorrectly believe that concerted efforts to teach black history and utilize Afrocentric resources will result in black youth who are too focused on race, overly pessimistic about whites, and thus ill-prepared to live and work in a predominately white world. But this belief could not be further from the truth! Racial pride has been shown to instill confidence and self-awareness in persons as well as promote interest in diverse groups and cultures.[4] Simply put, black youth who feel better about themselves are more likely to feel positively about other people! Black church youth ministries can use a variety of imaginative resources, programs, and activities to help black youth appreciate their ethnic cultural heritage and embrace this important dimension of their identity. Such endeavors represent another way to intentionally create both a culture of hope and content of hope for youth. Here are fifteen common (and less common) examples to consider:

1. Institute Black History Day, Week, and Month.

2. Introduce youth to some aspect of black history at every youth event. You can never provide too much information on this topic!

3. Plan and present a black history play for the congregation.

4. Place Afrocentric murals, pictures, and other artwork in rooms designated for youth ministry (and all around the church building).

5. Continually remind students that black history is actually American history. Teach them about the unique contributions made by blacks to the nation and the world.

6. Incorporate arts-related cultural traditions in youth ministry (for example, drum classes and storytelling).

7. Intentionally inform students about connections between African history and black history.

8. Incorporate Afrocentric resources in Bible studies (for example, the story of the Ethiopian eunuch) and practical teaching events (for example, ABEKA books).[5]

9. Remind students that all biblical characters were people of color. (See *The Original African Heritage Study Bible,* Cain Hope Felder, ed., from Judson Press.)

10. Expand youth repertoires by including material and practices about other ethnic groups, such as Latinos, Africans, Irish, Germans, Asian, American Indians, and Italians.

11. Include music forms historically associated with the black experience, such as jazz, blues, and Negro spirituals, in the curriculum.

12. Encourage students to create and perform their own rap or hip hop songs.

13. Honestly discuss sensitive, controversial topics, such as racism, discrimination, stereotypes, prejudices, classism,

sexism, and homophobia, in safe spaces and in nonjudgmental ways.[6]

14. Practice and role-play possible scenarios black youth may encounter and teach them how to live as change agents.

15. Constantly remind black youth that God loves them unconditionally and you love them unconditionally, and of why they should love themselves unconditionally.

Programs of promise must specifically and strategically socialize black youth to see the merits of black history, cultural diversity, and inclusivity. It may take additional time, effort, creativity, and intentionality for youth ministry leaders to incorporate Afrocentric themes and other resources in youth ministry. But only by doing so can we help cultivate well-rounded, racially healthy black youth who are best prepared to effect change in their own lives and in the lives of others.

When Disaster Strikes

The events of Hurricanes Katrina and Rita in Louisiana brought direct attention to the question, "What is required of youth ministry in the wake of devastating circumstances?" Life in our communities and in our churches does not always continue as we would like it. Natural disasters strike on occasion without warning and adequate preparation; and often, as was the case with Hurricanes Katrina and Rita, loss of life, homes, churches, and whole communities leave grief, loss of hope, and questions about how to move ahead. But as a New Orleans youth ministry leader put it, "Crisis can be anything, and people, including youth, experience all sorts of trauma." In discussions with pastors, youth leaders, and youth in New Orleans after their return, Vision Quest researchers learned what is hoped for and what is possible when tragedy strikes. These survivors offered some best practices to be welcomed for use by others in ministry with youth.[7]

We are in it together. The New Orleans leaders emphasized that it was all too easy to focus on the adults—their losses, disorganization, removal from familiar surroundings, deep feelings, and need for resources to reconstruct their own and their families' lives. But these results of the hurricanes were also felt by children and youth. The leaders underscored that for those who remain and for those who return, it is important to convey to youth with adults present that all are in it together—that they are not alone in their experiences.

Welcome the voices of the youth. The words of Rev. C brought light to the immediate need for youth to tell their stories: "Youth must be able to say, 'This hurts; this is frightening.' They must feel free to express their emotions without hiding them inside. The honest, authentic response of the leader must follow that 'we may have some rough hills to climb. I can't tell you for sure how things are going to play out. But I do know we're going to make it. Now tell me what would you like me and the church to do? What would you like to do?'" When these questions were posed to the youth, they responded by saying, "Start doing the things we did before Katrina. Like the Sunday school after church, the Christmastime events and the wonderful times we used to have." "Keep donating to whoever needs things here." "Let's keep sending things to Haiti like we did before 'cause we're not the only ones hurting."

Keep the church doors open. Rev. G said, "Lose the tendency to lock up the church for safekeeping. As leaders, we must think back about the deliverance of our forebears and our standing on their shoulders even now. They opened the doors to our future. It is up to us to open the doors to our youths' future in the wake of the storm. The doors of the church must be open to serve as a refuge and a place of solace and hope. But it must also face outward with our going out to where our youth and their families are."

Create community partnerships. The leaders agreed that the church's ability to address the needs of youth and their families in the wake of disaster or crisis happens only through the formation of a network made up of churches, pastors, community leaders, social workers, and school leaders. Efforts must be placed on creating a ministry map within a certain radius of the physical location of a church based on going out and locating and making contact with these resources. To use Rev. W's words, "We can't do it all by ourselves."

Instill hope. Rev. E made the point that "in rough situations like ours, there are some practical things that have to be done with our young people. We have to be with them as they work through their fears. But we have to instill in them that they have a destiny. God has a purpose for them. We need to set that bar and press them to strive for it. A program in my church called Y.E.S. (Youth Excelling and Strengthening) is designed to do just that."

Youth Speak on Outcomes to What's Happening

Youth ministry in our churches is about assuring youths' formation of knowledge, skills, experiences, aptitude, and self-efficacy to handle a myriad of situations they will inevitably face in the world. Importantly, this ministry is also about instilling in youth a transformative power that results in their "catching the spirit." This power comes through a personal relationship with God through Jesus Christ. When leaders have goals for youth ministry and programs to carry out the goals, our hope is that what we do will make a difference in the lives of youth; and the best way to discover what this impact is, is by asking youth to share it.

Conversations with youth from churches in the national study show that ministry with them and on their behalf has had an impact on their lives. In some cases, awareness surfaced that there are youth who want something better or different, grieve when a youth ministry leader leaves after a short stay, dislike the attitudes of adults, and have anger and sadness on being treated as outsiders. Youth who express these concerns must be heard and their concerns addressed. Other youth have quite a different response that showed in a variety of positive remarks. The encouraging words of youth point to what is hoped for on a large scale. In particular, youth gave attention to ways youth ministry has influenced their spiritual growth and views toward the church, resilience and hope, academic performance, service orientation, and life direction. "Listen in" now on some of their comments.

A "Yes" to Spiritual Growth and
Views toward the Church

Youth who shared their thoughts on how their involvement in youth ministry affected them positively were not shy in saying that their experiences enriched their relationship with God, informed their ways of behaving as Christians, and increased their desire to enter into the life of the church. Here is what they said:

- "My youth program has strengthened my relationship with God. Going to the different meetings, retreats, and service activities has brought me closer to God. Being in the youth program has taught me patience, respect, and tolerance of other people. There are always going to be people you do not like. But you have to learn to have respect for them and deal with them, or find a dignified way to discuss an issue with them. That's being Christian."

- "It gave me more knowledge of Christ. I know more about God than I ever did. Because of the program, I actually like coming to church."

- "The youth program has become more and more exciting; and now, instead of getting upset about going to church and Bible study, I can't wait until church starts. I've learned to take a backseat so that I can observe certain situations before I get involved in them. It has helped me to be more relaxed and less rambunctious."

- "My youth leader's kindness and leniency opened my eyes on how to live a good Christian life; and although I'm not there yet, I am consciously working on it."

In an additional story, a youth recalled a personal challenge that impacted his view toward church by saying: "Well, I remember when I wasn't really coming to church a lot. There was a moment in my life when I started high school and felt so overwhelmed with that, that I stopped coming. Then one day I started coming back, and instead of people looking at me like I was an outcast, everybody welcomed me back with open arms, saying, 'Where have you been? We missed you!' All that positive reinforcement made me feel like I belong here. It made me feel good about myself."

A "Yes" to Resilience and Hope

A dominant theme among youth is that it's hard to "stay up on it (or be fully present and attentive) when stuff keeps coming at you." However, for some, youth ministry has helped them form a helpful and hopeful perspective about themselves and life, as indicated in the following responses:

- "Well, I would say it's really helped me feel confident in myself, knowing that I can speak in front of the church and be a leader in the church. I can be somebody the other youth look up to. It really helped me to mold myself into a good leader."

- "The youth program has helped me stay positive. There are some things in this neighborhood that aren't positive, but the church kept me going. It keeps me connected. Really, my social skills and interacting with others have improved."

- "Attitude! It made it better; and knowledge too! I'm very aware of things I should and should not be doing. Self-esteem? I feel proud of myself. A whole lot of times, I did not want to go around certain people; but now I see that I am a better person and became a young man. My self-esteem has 'boosted up.'"

- "Well, it's kind of helped me with my skills and how to be a young man, and what a young man should do to survive in the world, basically."

A "Yes" to Academic Improvement

With staggering numbers of high school dropouts among black students, the historic role of the black church in encouraging educational achievement is a pivotal one today. For some youth, ministry with them has made a difference. Youth gave the following testimonies:

- "The pastor always asked me about my grades and how school was going. Before, I was always having issues; but now I am doing a lot better."

- "If I didn't have the Word, I probably wouldn't get the kinds of grades I get in school, not work as hard as I do in school 'cause I learned that 'I can do all things through Christ who strengthens me.' That comes up in my head all the time."

- "They (the pastor and the youth ministry leader) helped me get through at a time when I was having family problems and I couldn't express myself. I had issues in school that I couldn't tell anyone about. But my youth group leader talked to me, and I was able to let it all go in a short time frame. Things changed for the better."

- "My youth pastor called me in the office and prayed with me at a really hard time in my life, and put me in touch with a tutoring program. I would bring my homework in. My grades turned into As and Bs."

A "Yes" to Service

Involvement in community service projects contributed to the formation of a heart for service in several youth. Their comments were: "It changed my outlook in terms of community service. I really like giving back"; "I feel like I'm making a difference in the community, and that makes me feel better about myself"; and "Since we do a lot of community service, I'm more aware of what's going on around me now. I'm always looking for opportunities to give back."

The testimonies of youth present a "picture" of leaders and youth ministry that serve as instruments of transformation and hope. The testimonies show that leaders and youth ministry can be—must be—resources for youths' internal developmental assets in the form of moral and spiritual strength, positive attitudes, and abilities needed to confront life's realities.

The Challenge before Us

Hope-centered programs of promise are possible! No longer should they be pipe dreams for faith-filled yet frazzled youth ministry leaders! Our prayer is that the information provided in this chapter will help educate, equip, and empower youth ministry leaders. We close this chapter by drawing on points made in previous ones to present ten best practices that will move you closer to developing the hope-centered minister you know God has called you to be. Use these ten practices as self-reflection checkpoints.

✓CHECK IT OUT

Ten Best Practices for Hope-Centered Youth Ministry

1. *Leaders who fail to plan, plan to fail.* This statement may seem like a cliché, but it's true. Don't be afraid to fail (think outside the box and be creative, because youth expect newness and innovation). Don't be afraid to acknowledge when something didn't work. Every program, activity, or event may not have the intended effect. Learn from that experience. Identify and understand the major reasons it was unsuccessful and work to minimize a reoccurrence.

2. *The more the merrier.* Don't be afraid to ask for help. Involve as many interested people from the church and community as possible. Intentionally build church and community networks and alliances. Make sure persons will be committed to youth ministry and are willing, if needed, to be prepared. Sadly, some churches and ministries become so isolated that they undermine the ability to create adaptive, resilient youth programs of promise. Welcoming others to engage in youth ministry with you requires trust, willingness to share authority, and the ability to take a chance that others may do well or fail in their attempts to help.

3. *Listen to youth.* Studies show that black youth who are involved in the church are 34 percent more likely to report having a religious mentor who has been active in their lives since they were fourteen years old than youth who were less involved in church.[8] You can be that mentor! Many youth ministries fail because the adults in charge single-handedly determine every aspect of the ministry—from the mission to every program. Yet they are surprised when

youth do not flock to their planned events. Discerning youth ministry leaders are challenged to stop, look, and listen to youth. Proactively engage in
conversations to determine their needs and wants. This does not mean that
you acquiesce to your role as leader. Rather, acknowledge the importance
of getting their input. Tap into youth culture. Read youth magazines. Listen
to the types of music they do. Find out their interests and concerns, and you
will be better able to develop a responsive youth ministry. And by taking the
time to listen to youth, you are silently saying that you value their opinions as
much as you value them.

4. *Lead by example.* Don't be afraid to lead. Studies show that even when
youth act like they don't want boundaries and guidance, they secretly do.
Don't be afraid to be an assertive yet loving leader. Set parameters and ex-
plain them to youth. Clearly identify goals and objectives, and get their input
along the way. Youth will appreciate your attention and concern for their well-
being. Model the type of godly person you wish them to become.

5. *Engage in self-care.* It is not uncommon for a youth leader to experience
burnout. Commitment requires sacrifice, dedication, and service. It's a lot of
hard work! If not careful, a youth leader can become spiritually, emotionally,
psychologically, and physically exhausted. And a burned-out youth ministry
leader cannot help herself or himself or others. In addition, it is often difficult
to bounce back quickly from a case of chronic burnout. After reaching this
state, some youth ministry leaders simply exit their roles. Self-care means
taking time off to take care of oneself. It means being comfortable relying on
help from other youth ministry members to keep from being stretched too
thin. Taking vacations and weekends off, turning off the cell phone, saying no
to some requests—these are some of the things youth leaders must intentionally do during the self-care process. By taking time to become refreshed
and renewed, youth ministry leaders are insuring the ability to consistently
continue their calling to serve youth.

6. *Educate yourself formally and informally.* Programs of promise require
knowledge from a variety of sources. As noted in chapter 4, youth ministry
leaders are encouraged, if possible, to become formally prepared. But even
formally prepared youth leaders are encouraged to be open to learning and
obtaining information from alternative sources. Read mainstream books on
youth ministry. Attend conferences on the subject. Read studies from the

arenas of theology, black culture, organizational development, group dynamics, youth development, and black history. Listen to sermons and Bible studies about youth ministry and youth leadership on CDs and DVDs. These types of teaching/learning experiences will hone your skills and expand your knowledge base. As a youth leader for a hope-centered ministry, you can never learn enough about and for youth.

7. *Find a personal mentor.* As a youth ministry leader, people will come to you for advice, support, and guidance. For some youth leaders, it is difficult to acknowledge and seek out people to support, advise, and guide them. But locating a personal mentor is crucial. A personal mentor can help you restore hope when it may wane as a result of the rigors of youth ministry. This person may be from inside or outside your church. It should be someone with spiritual and practical wisdom and knowledge to help fortify and reenergize you as well as serve as an impartial sounding board.

8. *Get intangible and tangible resources.* Many youth ministry leaders focus all their attention on acquiring tangible resources for their respective ministries. Yes, budgets, volunteers, equipment, and snacks are necessary. However, equally necessary are intangible resources needed to cultivate a hope-centeredness. Be sure your youth ministry is filled with volunteers and staff who are loving, kind, supportive, nonjudgmental, and patient. Make sure they are willing to work as a team. Be sure they understand and support the ministry's vision and mission. Be sure they understand the power of the Holy Spirit and tap into this power base regularly for comfort, guidance, and support. Be sure they are actively striving to emulate Christ in their own lives. Be sure they are trained or open to being trained. Most of all, be sure they enjoy working with youth! To successfully develop programs of promise, intangible resources are just as critical as tangible ones.

9. *Visit model youth ministries.*[9] Given all the media attention about what youth and churches are doing wrong, it is refreshing to learn about congregations engaged in creative, successful holistic youth ministry. Find out whether such churches are located in your city or community. Visit them. Contact the pastor about establishing a youth ministry partnership. Minimally request a meeting with the youth ministry leader to garner information that may help your efforts. Exposure to model programs will reduce your reinventing the wheel and may provide fresh ideas to implement and challenges to avoid.

10. *Set high standards and expect (and strive) to exceed them!* God has given us God's best in the person of Jesus Christ. We are also challenged to give our best as youth ministry leaders. This means establishing high standards for your programs, practices, and processes. It requires faith in God, in yourself, in your ministry team, and in the youth you serve. Have high expectations for all those persons involved. And don't just work to meet your ministry goals and objectives—strive to exceed them—knowing that, with God, all things are possible!

NOTES

1. Findings from our study of churches where seminarians from historically black seminaries were leaders or affiliated with youth ministries indicate that 213 provide 1–11 youth programs, 8.9 percent (n=22) sponsor 12 or more youth programs, and 12 churches (5.6 percent) do not sponsor any youth programs. Programs refer to any sponsored youth ministry activity as shown in Table 7.1. The most reason for the absence of youth programs include lack of youth (5.3 percent), no or little interest by youth (2.8 percent), or no adult volunteers (2.0 percent). Churches with youth programs that are led by seminarians who are associate pastors (22.7 percent), lay youth leaders (18.8 percent), or youth pastors (13.6 percent) tend to sponsor 12 or more youth programs as compared to their peers with other types of leaders. When denomination is assessed, 45.4 percent, 22.7 percent, 18.2 percent, and 9.1 percent of AME, Baptist, COGIC, and UM churches, respectively, sponsor 12 or more programs. However, none of the CME, AMEZ, or Presbyterian churches sponsor 12 or more youth programs. Churches that sponsor 1–11 youth programs spend on average $7,126 annually. Yet those that sponsor 12 or more youth programs spend about $22,707 during that same period.

2. When denominations are considered, Baptist, COGIC, and AME churches tend to sponsor the most youth programs; CME and Presbyterian congregations tend to sponsor the least.

3. You are encouraged to read the following works: Cornel West, *Race Matters* (New York: Vintage, 1st edition, 1994); Joe R. Feagin, *Systemic Racism: A Theory of Oppression* (New York: Routledge, 2006); Joe R. Feagin, *The White Racial Frame: Centuries of Racial Framing and Counter-Framing* (New York: Routledge, 2010); and Eduardo Bonilla-Silva, *Racism without Racists: Color-Blind Racism and the Persistence of Racial Inequality in the United States* (Lanham, MD: Rowman & Littlefield, 2009).

4. See Cornel West, *Race Matters* (New York: Vintage, 1st edition, 1994).

5. A BEKA books is a publisher affiliated with Pensacola Christian College (PCC). This publisher produces Christian curricula for grades K–12.

6. See Sandra Barnes, *Subverting the Power of Prejudice: Resources for Individual and Social Change* (Downers Grove, IL: InterVarsity, 2006).

7. An excellent resource to consult is John D. Kinsel, "Working with Children and Adolescents after a Disaster," 261–85, in Stephen B. Roberts and Willard W. C. Ashley Sr., eds., *Disaster Spiritual Care: Practical Clergy Responses to Community, Regional and National Tragedy* (Woodstock, VT: Skylight Paths, 2008).

8. Lance D. Erickson and James W. Phillips, "The Effect of Religious-Based Mentoring on Educational Attainment: More Than Just a Spiritual High?" *Journal for the Scientific Study of Religion* 51, no. 3 (2012): 568–87.

9. Refer to Sandra Barnes, *Black Megachurch Culture: Models for Education and Empowerment* (New York: Peter Lang, 2010), for information on black megachurches with impressive youth ministries.

PART 3

Hope-Centered Youth Ministry Support

I pray that the God of our Lord Jesus Christ, the Father of glory,
may give you a spirit of wisdom and revelation as you come to know him,
so that, with the eyes of your heart enlightened,
you may know what is the hope to which he has called you,
what are the riches of his glorious inheritance among the saints,
and what is the immeasurable greatness of his power for us who believe,
according to the working of his great power.
–Ephesians 1:17-19

8

PARENT POWER

Parents as Hope-Builders

*You shall love the LORD your God with all your heart,
and with all your soul, and with all your might. Keep these
words that I am commanding you today in your heart.
Recite them to your children and talk about them when you
are at home and when you are away, when you lie down and
when you rise. Bind them as a sign on your hand, fix them
as an emblem on your forehead, and write them on the
door-posts of your house and on your gates.*
—Deuteronomy 6:5-9

Two-parent homes, single-parent homes, foster parent homes, adoptive parent homes, divorced parent homes, blended family homes, grandparent and other kin-headed homes—this full range of homes is represented among today's teens, including the ones in our youth ministry, congregations, and neighborhoods around our churches. In chapter 3, we referred to these homes as domains of the stories of which youth leaders should be aware in order to know the youth we serve. Youth ministry leaders also want and need support of parental figures to carry out excellent and hope-centered ministry. Leaders tell us, however, that this support often happens erratically; and in many instances, it is in short supply. The situation results in two critical questions raised by leaders: "Where are the parents?" and "Why aren't they here?" Youth ministry leaders raise these key questions because of the critical importance of parents in ministry with their youth.

When parental figures are involved, they form a relational partnership with youth ministry. Their awareness of what is going on in the lives of their youth and the awareness they gain about youth ministry open the way for shared guidance in their youths' Christian and personal identity formation. Parental involvement also forms a relational resource for youth ministry, which relies on parents for program assistance, overall youth encouragement, community outreach, and financial support. Surrogate parents within congregations also function as needed and helpful resources in youth ministry. Through their involvement in youth ministry, parents in the youths' homes or "other parents" in the church family join with youth ministry leaders and congregations in investing in the lives of black youth.[1] They contribute to a necessary collective process and bring parent power to bear on the hope-centered goal of forming young people who are Christian unapologetically and black unashamedly. In this chapter, we will consider kinds of parental involvement, ways of getting parents involved, and actions to take in the struggle to maintain parent power in youth ministry.

Parents as Hope-Building Partners in Youth Ministry

Youth ministry leaders in the Vision Quest study unanimously voiced the view that in whatever form parenting takes today, parents have a powerful role to play in the lives of their youth. For Christians, the role of parents as spiritual leaders in family life has been handed down in the Old Testament story of Moses' instruction to parents shown in the opening Scripture in this chapter. We read there that parents have the responsibility for communicating and modeling the faith to their children.[2] As part of the study, a group of today's black parents were asked to recall the spiritual role of their parents. Some of them told of very clear ways this duty was carried out by their parents when they were young: "We were definitely going to eat meals together, say grace, and repeat Bible verses before meals. We went to Sunday school and church together. No one was left behind. At least one of our parents made sure we got to youth group meetings. Parents prepared food for our meetings. But for holidays like Halloween, Christmas, and Easter, everybody came together and sang, played games, and fellowshipped together." The interesting part of this kind of sharing was the follow-up, because almost without any difference among them, the parents told a different story of what happens today.

The dominant story of today's parents seems to be one of hectic busyness for every family member and of pressures that make life difficult. Present-day parents continue to feel a war that is being waged against them by the economy, as well as by family and social issues.[3] One parent said, "Time to eat together? Well, no! Not a lot! Are there other times for family members to get together? It's difficult to plan. Getting my child to youth group? I have to say that he prefers to go with his friends. So I don't go. I let him go on his own." Other parents say they would like to do more than they are doing in the lives of their children, but they feel inadequate to do it well, given their circumstances.

Parents and leaders alike say they don't see the end of the current trend of family relational patterns and issues like those described. But neither are they ready to say that the entire picture is bleak. There are a variety of patterns of parental involvement in youth ministry from "wait and see" parents to fully engaged parents. These patterns evolve from decisions made by parents based on their unique needs and interests. These patterns also affirm that there is no singular, universally accepted, or best parent involvement role. There is room for an array of parental involvement patterns. Even as youth ministry leaders in the Vision Quest national study desire more parental involvement, the very real and widely ranging circumstances of parents and families today must prompt leaders to be alert and sensitive to real reasons for the range of responses and open to explore what might be done to alleviate the challenge of parental involvement. The patterns include the following:

• *Wait and see parents.* Some parents who are members of congregations take a "wait and see" position as they and their teens discern what is best to do in light of their personal situations and needs. They take their time to consider the benefits of youth ministry for their teens or what or how much is actually possible for them to commit to based on their circumstances. In this "wait and see" posture, both the parents and their teens may attend church regularly or periodically but refrain from making a commitment to youth ministry involvement. Because of their personal situations or other reasons, a parent may also come to church worship without the teen or the teen without a parent. A senior pastor confessed, "I share information about youth ministry from the pulpit. But, I know that there's an unspoken answer of 'Not now,' when I don't see the youth and the parents at youth events." However, this pastor recognizes that moving parents and even their teens beyond the "wait and see" posture doesn't happen according to the pastor's desire and timetable. And, in fact, it shouldn't happen this way.

Addressing the big question of the role of the pastor may be answered at least in part by the following: Continue to share pertinent information and let all youth and parents know that they are welcome to participate. Act on the message of Rev. T in Chapter 3 that it is important to connect personally with both the youth and their parents. This connection may be made through pastoral visits in their homes as means of becoming aware of the family's everyday environment and of letting them know that the church really cares and represents a God who cares for people.

• *"Back off" parents.* Parents take a "back off" approach to youth ministry. They believe their teens need time with peers away from the presence and oversight of parents. One parent explained it by saying, "It's important for my kids to have a place to go. I'm glad it's the church. They're into it. That's great! I don't think I need to be present. I think it's my place to 'back off.' I don't get involved in it."

• *Partial involvement parents.* Because of the busy schedules of many of today's parents, it is necessary for them to make decisions about the kinds of involvement they can comfortably and appropriately undertake. These parents support their teens' active participation in the church's youth ministry and show delight when opportunities for public leadership and performance are given to their teens or the whole youth group. On these occasions that often happen on Youth Sunday or at special events, busy parents carve out time to be proud supporters or cheerleaders to the youths' achievement. These parents consider this partial involvement role as essential and non-negotiable. It is the right thing to do in light of their circumstances.

• *Behind the scenes parents.* Some parents are present but choose to remain in the background or fulfilling a behind the scenes role. They describe themselves as being "supporters in the wings" in the interest of not interfering with the activities of the youth. These parents tend to know what is going on in youth ministry. One parent expressed it like this: "I think it's my responsibility to know what my teen is being exposed to. That doesn't mean I'm sitting in a youth group meeting and taking over things. No, it's nothing like that! Kids have to be able to have their say. But I'm on the premises. I help prepare the food, help get the games out for the recreation period, or do any other preparation that might be needed for activities; but I don't stay around. For me, that's just the way it is." In short, the "behind the scenes parents" see their particular pattern of involvement as important to the youths' developing a sense of their independence.

• *Available when needed parents.* In some instances, parents have said: "If there's a program, field trip, or lock-in where chaperones are needed, count me in." These parents make it clear that they are available to respond to requests for help when needed; and help may lead to providing group mentoring and monitoring or intervening in disciplinary matters when called upon to do so.

• *Fully engaged parents.* Full engagement describes the role of parents or guardians who serve as youth ministry leaders. This parental role as leader often happens when parents have children who reach the age for youth ministry involvement and leadership is not available. However, there are also occasions when parents without teens volunteer or when parents continue as leaders after their children leave. References to the calling of these parents appeared in chapter 1. A variation of fully engaged parents is found in those who are not youth ministry leaders but who show up for every event, bring other children with them, engage in outreach, and provide financial support for youth ministry.

✓CHECK IT OUT

How would you describe the involvement of parents in your youth ministry? Who are the parents? How many participate, and in what capacity? What key factors contribute to their involvement or difficulty in participation?

Today's black youth cry for a sense of belonging that they can feel and claim with caring others. They search for it in youth ministry. They want it from their parents. As Tara put it, "Our parents' role is to get us to the church and to different events. But it's more than that. We also have to have their support. If they're not going to support us, then who will? They need to get involved. Like, we ought to see them interested in what we're doing and come out to help us and sometimes hear what we've got to say. And, something else, like, while we're doing the car wash to raise funds for a trip, parents ought to come out to support us. Okay, that goes for playing a role in all our activities." Eric said, "Everyone should share the leadership. Parents should be involved. Sometimes we youth don't have a voice. We should have a voice. But parents shouldn't have to be quiet either." Sierra interrupted, "Well, parents shouldn't be around all the time. We have to have a chance to be by ourselves. How else will we be able to learn what it takes to grow up? I'll say this though. An adult asked me if I want to be raised by my peers. I said, 'No!'"

These and other youth shared a point that must not be forgotten: parents must not be left out. An inescapable role of ministry leaders is building, affirming, and empowering much-needed relationships with parents for the sake of their children. These relationships can foster well-being, emotional adjustment, a positive outlook on life, and spiritual anchoring in tough times. Youth need these relationships, and youth ministry is a place where these relationships can be fostered.[4] How can we create the necessary partnership between parents and youth ministry?

Create Partnership Awareness

Youth ministry leaders and congregational leaders need to recognize that relevant programming, youth participation, and parental support are related to one another, as shown in figure 8.1. The importance of this connectedness must also be shared with parents and the larger church family. We want parents to see their role, own their role, and act on it.

In order to share with parents the message about their important role as partners, ministry leaders must make contact with them. It isn't enough to make announcements from the pulpit on Sundays or include a paragraph in the church newsletter. Effective communication is more personal than that. In chapter 2, we drew attention to home visits as a way for leaders to connect with and come to know youth. This manner of connecting also creates an opening for contact with parents. Awareness continues through specific actions that include embracing parents, informing parents, and empowering parents through open communication. Communication is a key activity!

Embrace parents through open communication. A helpful approach is for youth ministry leaders to invite parents to attend an

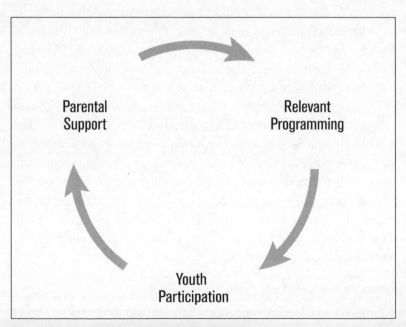

Figure 8.1. The interdependent youth ministry.

informal gathering after church not just to talk about youth ministry but, most importantly, to get to know them and inquire about their needs. In meetings of this kind, leaders become aware of who the parents are. These gatherings offer excellent opportunities for discovery of parental concerns, interests, and gifts. These meetings also send a message that ministry with youth is a family affair and promotes the development of a village. Creating a village involves fostering relational ties for support of youths' well-being and Christian formation. As parents, grandparents, and other guardians come together and begin to recognize common struggles and interests, a natural supportive bond forms. They begin to communicate with each other and uncover their own interconnectedness. A bond also begins to be created between the youth ministry leader and parents as the leader communicates to parents the hospitable qualities of *Sawubona* ("I see you") mentioned in chapter 5. These qualities focus on openness to hear what parents have to say. When leaders act on these qualities, we may discover specific kinds of responses to parents that will increase the likelihood of their partnering with youth ministry. For example, we may find that parent partnering depends on the following:

- Youth ministry programming schedules that coincide with other church events that parents already attend, such as choir rehearsals or activities for married couples or single parents.

- Provision of child care for younger siblings of teens when parents' presence is needed for youth ministry events.

- Making parents aware of places or venues for youth ministry activities beyond the church so that parents can negotiate travel distances and time management in light of other family responsibilities.

- Creating family-focused events, combining youth ministry efforts with other ministries of the church in a single, intergenerational event. This increases the potential for parent partnering when the entire family can come, reducing multiple trips for parents and child care concerns.

Inform parents through open communication. Keeping parents informed may seem like a daunting task. However, it is a major part of youth ministry and must be carried out if parents are to become committed youth ministry partners. Providing ongoing updates to parents about events and timelines of youth ministry programs and activities is particularly important. Presenting parents with as much information as possible about youth ministry activities is essential, particularly in light of the overextended nature of today's family life. Providing event and scheduling information in advance by e-mail, phone, texts, person-to-person contacts, e-newsletters, information call-in lines, church bulletins, church websites, flyers, banners, and postcards allows families to include youth ministry events on their calendars and to plan for them.

Empower parents through open communication. When leaders share with parents a personal vision and passion for youth ministry, we create a platform for parents to envision their role in the ministry. A leader's vision and excitement about ministry with the parents' children can be contagious. Parents can catch the importance of this ministry undertaking from us, and this contagion can become an empowering force in their response of *Sikhona* ("I am here") to our *Sawubona* ("I see you") hospitality extended to them. Vision sharing also gives permission to parents to situate themselves in a particular task in youth ministry.

Parents do not get involved in youth ministry if they feel inadequately prepared to take part, but they also fail to take on roles if they don't know what sort of help they might give or aren't approached to help. We can empower them by communicating a variety of specific ways from which parents may choose to become partners according to their interests, skills, and time availability. For example, leaders may present the following ways parents may become partners:

- Become a prayer partner. Engage in daily prayer on behalf of youth ministry, the youth involved in it, and those who lead it.

- Help with food donations, preparation and/or serving.

- Be a chaperone on trips and at lock-ins.

- Help lead activities.

- Engage in fund-raising.

- Encourage youth by attending ministry events like worship led by youth or other special occasions on which they are present or are honored.

- Engage in outreach to recruit new youth and parents.

Parents or other adults raising teens may not get involved in youth ministry because of difficult relational issues with their teens. They need and seek help in relating to their youth. Youth ministry can go a long way in responding to this need by offering parenting activities, workshops, or seminars. When parents experience a rise in the kind of relational aptitude that is desirable for youth ministry leaders, they are more inclined to become ministry partners.

The Save Our Sons (SOS) program in Florida is an example of youth ministry programming that was designed to address the issue of parenting. Specifically, the initiative sought to help parents and other adults raising teens learn or refresh parent to teen relational skills. The ministry invites parents to attend interaction skills-building sessions during the same time period the youth are involved in their activities. Professionals from community organizations lead sessions on parenting, services that are available to them in their community, and other activities that may be of interest to parents and their family life. SOS also stresses their expectation and hope that parents will avail themselves of this opportunity instead of "dropping the youth off and leaving."

The Church as Family

We were reminded at the beginning of this chapter that what constitutes a family varies. No matter the family structure, youth programs can represent critical *proxy families* for youth who, for various reasons, do not have stable, positive home lives. In this instance, thinking outside the box means recognizing that youth ministry may mean far more than weekly Bible studies and rap sessions. For some youth, it may be the closest thing to home and family they have! A thoughtful youth minister must "know" her or his youth membership and information about their home lives and personal challenges. Garnering this information will mean really listening to youth and also listening to the many unspoken ways youth attempt to communicate their needs, desires, and concerns. By doing this, youth ministry leaders can create a home away from home for which so many youth yearn. An outcome of this kind of programming may help youth understand what constitutes a family and help shape their expectations and decisions for the type of family they want to be a part of as adults.

To further emphasize the need for other "parents," Rev. D, a youth ministry leader, shared the following observation: "We are facing an epidemic of struggling families. So we have to reinvent family in order to embrace, encourage, and redirect young people who are basically directing themselves at home and in everyday life matters. We have to become family so our youth know that there is someone out there pulling for them." Rev. D continued, "As if the picture of families in general is not enough, the case of absent fathers in the lives of young men is a real hot issue. Fathers? We have to be that 'father' or find someone who will be present as 'father' and will push these young men forward. . . . Our young women need fathers, too, who affirm who they are and model male behavior that values and respects females."

Rev. D brought up another issue that must be faced: "A lot of our young people don't have parents that go to church with them. They don't have grandparents who come to church with them. There are instances when teens ask to be baptized and, no matter how great your appeal is, their parents don't show up. In those cases, other 'parents' step in and help. They love whoever needs love. They do whatever needs to be done. They help with youth ministry leadership in whatever way they can. Together, these 'parents' and I form a family and become family where parents are missing in order to bring love, guidance, and healing. This reality has brought to me the view of a model that goes beyond parents as we understand them. Rather than a parent model, it seems to me that we need a family model." Recruiting other "parents" and developing village-fostering programs can help to re-create family for youth.

✓ CHECK IT OUT

Consider the need for other "parents" in your church's youth ministry. Who already functions as surrogate parents in your church's youth ministry? How did they become involved? Who would you name as potential surrogate parents? What role(s) would you want them to fulfill?

Making Parent Power Come Alive

Getting and keeping parents involved requires intentional effort. A part of this endeavor entails the youth ministry leader's creation of a database of youth and their parents or guardians. Once you have it compiled, make sure to keep the information current. Use this database to stay in contact with both the youth and their parents or guardians. Make calls and home visits. When families know leaders are interested in them, their interest in youth ministry will grow.

Another helpful undertaking is to make a plan for parents' involvement. This plan entails creating a parents-in-action process so that leaders and parents know what is needed from parents and when. An Action Plan Worksheet like the one shown in figure 8.2 may be used to carry out the process.

ACTION PLAN			
Desired Outcome:			
Needed Actions:			
Already in Place (Or needs building on)	Action Steps	Who Is Responsible (Individual[s], group[s])	When (Beginning and desired end)
Work Group Members:			
Date:			

Figure 8.2. Action plan worksheet.[5]

Action Amid Continuing Struggle

Even after youth ministry and congregational leaders have done all that seems to be humanly possible to enlist parents as hope-building partners in youth ministry, we need not be surprised if the struggle continues. The challenges faced by today's families are real! Be aware of these challenges and the effect they have on parental involvement. Awareness provides some understanding of the real reasons for the range of responses presented earlier and offers a means of assessing what might be done to alleviate the challenges. Review chart 8.1 at right, which shows challenges and their impact on parents, youth, and youth ministry. Consider ways in which the contents of the chart apply to your situation.

Excellent, hope-centered youth ministry has the ability to reach youth and to serve as a unique ground for our youths' Christian and personal identity formation. The role of parents in this task is an important one, and yet we know that taking on a role is not always easy. However, when the effort is made, positive outcomes result. So let this effort begin!

✓ CHECK IT OUT

Either alone or in conversation with congregational leaders and one or more parents, reflect on the following:

- What kinds of involvement of parents in your youth ministry make you proudest?

- What is yet needed in empowering parents to become partners in your ministry with youth?

- Based on your reading of this chapter, what actions will you take to make parent power come alive in your youth ministry?

Chart 8.1. Effects of Family Struggles on Youth Ministry

Challenge	Effect on Parent	Effect on Youth	Effect on Ministry
Time Commitment	Parents now have less time than ever because of busy daily schedules.	Youth are unsupervised for extended periods of time, opening the window for additional challenges.	Participation of youth and ministry needs of youth may increase, but there may be no parental involvement.
Economy	The downturn in the economy means lost jobs, lost wages, underemployment, and lower earnings.	Youth may have to assist in carrying financial responsibility, which means they have less time for youth activities.	Youth ministry attendance may decrease, as well as financial support to programs. Stress reduces interest in parental involvement.
Extracurricular Activities	Youth activities in and beyond school come with significant financial investments and/or promise of future payoff.	Youth have to decide between participating in extracurricular activities and ministry opportunities or extend themselves to both.	Youth and parents may show a lack of commitment to satisfying financial and activity responsibilities.
Changing Community	Finding suitable or affordable housing or moving to communities zoned for better schools have emptied communities around the church.	Remaining youth show lack of interest where there are few youth participants. Relocated youth show lack of interest in joining a new ministry.	A decrease in quality programming may result, as well as less parental and youth participation.
Transportation	Transportation issues challenge those living long distances from a preferred church.	When getting to youth activities is difficult, youth are unable to commit to or to be consistent with the program.	Youth participation and parental involvement are hampered when transportation is a problem.
Lack of Relevant Programs	Poor programming hinders interest of parents.	Stagnant growth and low participation result when programs don't interest youth.	When programming is seen as not being worthwhile, youth participation will be low, and parents may not participate at all.

NOTES

1. Janelle J. Dance, *Tough Fronts: The Impact of Street Culture in Schooling* (New York: Routledge Falmer, 2002), cited in Shawn A. Ginwright, *Black Youth Rising: Activism and Radical Healing in Urban America* (New York: Columbia Univ. Press, 2010), 76. Ginwright draws on the work of Dance, who describes the kind of investment in building relationships with black youth called "the power of humane investments," in which the investor sees and makes possible more in youth than they see in themselves.

2. Merton P. Strommen and Richard A. Hardel, *Passing On the Faith: A Radical New Model for Youth and Family Ministry* (Winona, MN: Saint Mary's, 2000), 27–28. Strommen and Hardel also highlight the role of parents as spiritual leaders in family life as modeled by Moses in Israel's life.

3. Sylvia Ann Hewlett and Cornel West, *The War against the Family: What We Can Do for America's Beleaguered Moms and Dads* (Boston: Houghton Mifflin, 1998), 257. In the late 1990s, Hewlett and West wrote about these factors impinging on family life.

4. The importance of connections between parental relationships and youth and family ministry are made by Strommen and Hardel, *Passing On the Faith*, 20–24, 47–51; and by Almeida M. Wright, "The Power of Testimonies: Spiritual Formation and Ministering with Youth," 182–95, in Mary Elizabeth Moore and Almeda M. Wright, eds., *Children, Youth, and Spirituality in a Troubling World* (St. Louis, MO: Chalice, 2008), 189.

5. According to Strommen and Hardel, the Action Plan format was developed by the Youth and Family Institute of Augsburg College and called VisionPak. The format is found in Merton P. Strommen and Richard A. Hardel, *Passing On the Faith*, 305.

9

VILLAGE POWER
The Congregation as Hope-Builder

You show that you are a letter from Christ,
the result of our ministry, written not with ink
but with the Spirit of the living God, not on tablets
of stone but on tablets of human hearts.
—2 Corinthians 3:3

Whew! What a day! These thoughts race through fourteen-year-old Jamal's mind as he sprints out the front door of the tiny apartment he shares with his father and three brothers and sister. As the oldest, Jamal is responsible for many of the household chores—cooking, washing dishes, cleaning up the bathroom, babysitting his usually well-behaved but sometimes bratty siblings, and helping them with their homework. Still Jamal maintains an A average in advance-placement courses. Jamal doesn't mind the hard work; he's been trying to take some of the load off his father, who works nights as a custodian. *Boy! Have things changed since Ma died two years ago!* he thinks. Jamal does his part to help maintain some semblance of normality for his father, brothers, and sister. No, he doesn't mind.

But sometimes Jamal gets down when he thinks about things—his mother and why she died, how his father and siblings are coping, what will happen to his family without her, and about his future. But Jamal smiles and thinks, *I'd probably go crazy if it weren't for*

Ms. Foster and the St. Paul youth ministry! They are helping him make it through tough times. Jamal hurriedly runs down the street toward St. Paul—his siblings in tow. He is excited about what Ms. Foster has planned for them this week. Not only are they sure to have fun and good food, but they always talk about things that are important to Jamal. Ms. Foster has listened many times as Jamal has confided in her about his feelings. She seems to really understand. And she always reminds him that God is looking out for him—and so is the entire church family. This gives Jamal hope. As he scurries through the church door, Jamal knows everything will be all right. God has promised it!

Standing on the Promises

Like Jamal, youth in general and black youth in particular face many challenges daily. Sometimes their problems may seem small to adults. But to some youth, their problems are earth-shattering! Scholars like Andrew Billingsley[1] show that black families have and continue to effectively champion the needs and concerns of black children. Yet they don't do it alone. The historic black church has played an indelible role in the lives of black youth. A widely acclaimed 1990 study report, *The Black Church in the African American Experience* by C. Eric Lincoln and Lawrence H. Mamiya reminds us that, in fact, without the church, real hope for positive black consciousness and ongoing existence across the years would have been impossible.[2] Because of the church's role in black life, studies show that even now black youth are more likely to regularly attend church and participate in church-sponsored youth groups throughout high school than their white, Hispanic, and Asian counterparts.[3]

Black churches today have the shoulders of a powerful historic legacy to stand on; and they must build on the promise this legacy holds for today! As in the past, our churches must continue to be a primary mechanism to educate, equip, and empower black youth like Jamal. In earlier chapters, we highlighted that programs of promise must be undergirded by congregations, clergy, communities, and parents. The programs of promise described in chapter 7 are essential to black youth development! But these programs and the youth in them require congregations to be supportive, hope-building villages. There must be evidence of "village power" if youth ministry is to be a transforming resource for youth.

This chapter explores what a hope-building village looks like and what it takes to build and maintain it. We will focus attention on the kind of relational know-how, or relational aptitude, a congregation needs as a means of demonstrating "village power." Moreover, we will look at the importance of the congregation's operational know-how, or operational aptitude, in assuring excellent, hope-centered youth ministry.

Making Good on the Congregation's Relational Aptitude

Truth be known, there are some struggles in today's congregations that must be overcome. In chapter 8, we highlighted the vital role of parents, guardians, and volunteers in our churches' youth ministry that must come alive in new ways. But the role of congregations goes beyond the role of these ministry supporters. As one youth ministry leader said, "We need our congregations to be 'open door' communities that welcome the youth who are here and the ones not here." Or, as another youth leader said, "The village is broken down. We need everybody—the moms, dads, aunts, uncles, and grandparents, the whole extended family—working together with young people. Ministers and churches need to work together. It's not about you and your church. Look around the community. There are a lot of youth. We must embrace them too." We need the *Sawubona* church that was described in chapter 5. Recall that making it happen means engaging in some specific kinds of imagining and building processes that assure a *Sawubona* church. Yet we want to add here some know-how that reflects positive *relational functions* or a village mind-set and spirit. There are at least seven key steps to assess these functions.

Step one. Take a look at your congregational culture. Let's begin by looking at our congregations as a culture. Look around. See, hear, and feel what is going on. Notice that the congregation you are in is made up of a recognizable group of people. It has a particular way of going about its life. It has a tradition—a history. It carries out worship in a distinctive way. It has a particular understanding of the Christian faith and a set of beliefs it holds to. Particular activities are taking place in it. We can describe our congregational culture in terms of its location, the physical environment, and its symbols and artifacts. We feel it on the basis of the attitudes and expressed emotions of the members. Our congregations have preferences and decide on what's important based on those preferences. All of this makes each of our congregations a culture.

Youth ministry leaders must deal with the congregational culture by becoming aware of what it is like for youth to be part of the culture, or in fact, if they really are welcomed in it. As leaders, we observe, listen intently, enter into conversation about, and seek answers to questions we raise based on what we see, hear, and feel. But it is also important for congregational leaders to engage in the same process for the sake of looking at the place and importance of youth ministry in the church. How every aspect of the congregational culture connects with youth and the manner in which youth connect with it matters. The effort of a congregation to promote and support hope-centered, relational youth ministry is about making good on the congregation's relational aptitude. Engaging in periodic times of congregational self-review is an important way of assessing it.

Step two. Consider your church location. Where is your church located? Who lives near it? How would you describe the area, its residents, and its needs? Who are the youth, and are there few, many, or none who come to or are part of your church? What other organizations and facilities are located nearby (e.g., what other churches, schools, community centers, and/or recreational facilities)? Are these places where youth can be seen, heard, and reached? How may or does the presence of these facilities influence what your church does regarding youth ministry? Can alliances with these facilities be strategically used to create or advance your church's being or becoming a welcome place for youth and youth ministry?

Step three. Recall your church history. What is the history of your church? How did your church come to be in its present location? What past efforts to attract and retain youth are part of the church's documented history? Who are the church historians who can provide the story of your congregation's past? What are some of the historical turning points or some of the milestones in your church's history, and how have they influenced whether and how your church welcomes youth? How many youth have historically participated in your church, and in what capacity? If youth participation has waned, what were the reasons?

Step four. Review your member migration. Does your church maintain membership migration records? What are the ages, membership tenure, education, attendance patterns, and volunteer patterns? In what zip codes do most of the members live? Are most persons who attend Sunday services members or nonmembers? How far do they travel to get to church? Can you connect membership patterns to church efforts to welcome visitors, youth, and families of youth?

Step five. Assess your attitudes toward churched and unchurched youth. Who are the youth in your church? What are their needs? Are there any unchurched youth who attend your church? If so, how many and from what areas do they come? What are the attitudes toward churched and unchurched youth? Are distinctions made between the two groups? How do the pastor, other clergy, leaders, and parents feel about these two groups of youth? If different opinions exist, what are they? How do their opinions affect youth ministry? What do unchurched youth do on Sunday or when the youth groups meet? What effort is made to welcome them?

Step six. Evaluate your congregation at worship. What is a typical worship service like? In what ways are youth involved in worship? If they are not involved, where are they and why? What would you say are the youths' attitudes and feelings about worship in your congregation? Why? What efforts have been made to respond to youths' interests, desires, or requests for worship styles? What understandings would you say youth in your church have of the church's architecture (e.g., its seating arrangement, entrance, windows, pulpit, altar). What efforts are made to build understanding? What difference does it make to the youth, or to what extent do you think it should matter?

Step seven. Consider how you grow faith-filled leaders and disciples of Jesus Christ. How does your church convey revered tenets of the faith in ways that youth are eager to receive them?[4] How do you highlight and celebrate the maturity of youth as they grow into disciples of Jesus Christ and demonstrate leadership in and beyond the church? For example, which of the following rites of passage are carried out in your congregation and what would you add to the list?

- believers' baptism

- confirmation

- personal testimonies

- honors and awards for service

In addition, which of the following opportunities for youth leadership formation and discipleship development exist and what opportunities would you add to the list?

- appointment as a junior deacon or lay-leader

- service as worship leader

- service as preacher on Youth Sunday or other times

- service as an usher

- service as an acolyte

- Sunday school apprentice or assistant

- involvement in community service

Some key thoughts on youth and the worshipping community. Much diversity exists in the place and role of youth in the worshiping community. Some congregations support the separation of youth from Sunday morning worship experiences. In these instances, a Youth Church convenes in a designated location. These congregations often hold a Youth Sunday, whereby youth are the primary leaders in an intergenerational worship setting. In other instances, more than one worship service is offered, each with a differing worship style. Still other congregations carry out a unified intergenerational worship with opportunities for youth to serve in a variety of capacities. In order to assure the appeal of the worship style to all, these churches utilize youth in every aspect of worship or incorporate "out of the box" expressions, such as spoken word, drama, mime, liturgical dance, stepping, and drumming, as indicated in examples of best practices in chapter 7.[5]

It is important for congregations to discuss openly the range of options for the place and role of youth in the worshiping community, the pros and cons of each option, the option they choose, and their rationale for that choice. For example, adherents of a separate youth worship experience highlight the importance of assuring a youth-friendly worship experience as well as ongoing intentional and focused opportunities for leadership formation and discipleship development. Congregations who do not select this option raise concern that youths' fullest understanding of the unity of the body of Christ described in 1 Corinthians 12:12-31 is jeopardized. In other instances, congregations express a desire for designated times for a separate Youth Church so that a balance between youth-friendly worship and unity of the body of Christ may be achieved. Of course, one pastor said, "If we had the space needed for a Youth Church, we would do it. Without an available space, we can't consider it."

The use of more than one worship service in congregations allows for differing worship styles that appeal to various ages/stages. However, others move in another direction based on their biblical understanding "that there should be no division in the body, but that its parts should have equal concern for each other" (1 Corinthians 12:25). At the same time, congregations recognize that carrying out one or more worship services is demanding on the pastoral staff. Consequently, decisions are made with these demands in mind.

Congregations that hold to a unified intergenerational worship rely on a belief about the meaning of the family of God. For example, one pastor said, "We have to be the family God called us to be. We learn to be that family when we are together and worship together. Today, everybody goes in different directions during the week. At least we can come together on Sunday! That's not too much to ask! Anyway, Scripture also tells us that every member of the body is important (1 Corinthians 12:12-26)." At the same time, pastors tell of considering and comparing other forms with the unified intergenerational worship model. Weighing the options often comes from observations that the needs and interests of the diverse group of worshipers are not being fully met. In making the decision for or against unified intergenerational worship, it is important for congregations to consider the other options available to them and to reflect on whether or how the congregation demonstrates the following beliefs and values of intergenerational worship:

- In intergenerational worship, the church family passes on the faith to youth (Deuteronomy 6:7; 12:7; Joel 2:15-16).

- In intergenerational worship, the church family welcomes youth (Luke 18:15-17).

- In intergenerational worship, the church family recognizes the gifts of each generation to one another and that the generations cannot exist without the others (1 Corinthians 12:12-26).

✓ CHECK IT OUT

Assessing and then addressing your village are critical activities in taking seriously your congregation's relational aptitude. When it is done, congregations demonstrate their responsibility in intentionally seeing, reaching, and hearing youth, which is a precursor to cultivating welcoming, hope-centered youth ministries. In the absence of considering what is or is not being done to cultivate welcoming *Sawubona* spaces, youth will probably not come—and your church will lose its relevance among youth and in the larger community. We encourage youth ministry committees or advisory bodies in congregations to consider the earlier mentioned seven key steps to assessing your congregation's relational aptitude functions. Each one of the seven steps is important to excellent hope-centered youth ministry.

In your assessment process, go back and revisit especially suggestions highlighted in previous chapters on seeing and responding to youth not simply within your church walls but beyond. Congregations and youth leaders together are pivotal agents in addressing the unique needs of black youth who are members of our congregations, relatives of members who attend, and nonattending youth residing in the surrounding community. Community in-reach and outreach continue to be key twin requirements for assisting black youths' ability to make healthy choices, avoid risky behaviors, and grow up healthy, spiritually strong, educationally prepared, socially self-assured, resilient in the face of difficulty, and able to be positive contributors to the church and world. Congregations and leaders together are needed to see and build on youths' gifts and strengths and to assure their surviving and thriving in today's and tomorrow's world.

Remember that other outcomes may also result from the church's outreach. A youth ministry leader in a fairly small ministry in Tennessee attributes a lot of their group's growth to community outreach. The leader testified, "We've done a lot of evangelistic things in the community. We've reached out and we've reached a lot of young people from the community. Because we have included the youths' parents in our outreach, some of their parents have joined the church." By developing a family-oriented evangelical canvassing process, this church has been able to effectively attract youth and many of their parents from the surrounding area. Despite limited congregant numbers, their efforts show that such success happens through a clear ministry vision, an outreach plan, welcoming spaces, and a *faithful few*.

Another sometimes unspoken concern is congregations' outreach to post–high school and college-aged youth. An important question is "Does your church have programs for post–high school and college-aged youth?" Not all students leave town after they graduate from high school. Many attend local colleges or universities or enter the workforce. Nevertheless, they are often the most overlooked church demographic. A 2006 update by the Barna Group tells of most youth putting Christianity on the shelf after high school.[6] Given this staggering statistic, what is your congregation doing about youth who are part of this group? What ministries are in place to address their needs?

Making Good on the Congregation's
Operational Aptitude

An excellent, hope-centered youth ministry is grounded in the spiritual realm. However, certain very real steps must be taken to help insure its success from the time of inception and periodically and systemically throughout the ministry. Attention to the congregation's relational aptitude is one way of entering into those steps. But there are other church dynamics that can influence youth ministry. These dynamics are in the category called *internal church operational functions*. These functions are about how congregations support and facilitate youth ministry programs, activities, and leadership of this ministry.

Pivotal areas of support include the church's provision of material resources, such as the church's physical environment or activity spaces and equipment; financial support for leaders' salaries and continuing preparation; and financial assistance for youth ministry activities. Of these pivotal areas, the greatest challenge is in the area of financial resources. In fact, more than half (59.7 percent) of the participants in the Vision Quest national survey identified financial resources as a primary challenge to effective youth ministry leadership. In addition, the survey of black congregations showed that the average amount spent annually on youth ministries is about $8,361 and differs dramatically based on denomination:

- COGICs ($21,555)
- Baptists ($13,165)
- AMEZ ($11,000)
- Presbyterians ($7,186)
- AMEs ($3,368)
- UMCs ($3,440)
- CMEs ($823)

The survey revealed that congregations in the best financial health report expending about $19,276 annually on youth programs.

Financial resources clearly need priority attention. However, it is important that church leaders engage in periodic times of congregational self-review of every area of its operational aptitude for the sake of coming to grips with the extent of the congregation's promotion and support of youth ministry and ways to improve it. Helpful key questions for open and critical reflection focus attention on the following areas:

The church's physical environment. What are the available spaces for youth to meet? Do these spaces promote teaching, learning, relational activities, and recreation? Are they accessible to youth with physical limitations?

The church's budget. What is the church's overall budget, and how much of it is allocated for youth ministry in comparison to other ministries of the church?

The support of the youth ministry leader(s). What wage or other compensation is given to the youth ministry leader(s)?

The support of youth ministry programs and activities. What financial resources are allocated for teaching/learning materials and equipment? Programs and activities? Community outreach? Field trips? Technology supports?

✓CHECK IT OUT

It is important for church leaders to engage in full discussion on each one of the operational topics. In follow-up to your conversation, answer the questions:

- What material and financial support is provided by your church for youth ministry? From this support, what is beneficial to your youth ministry and youth ministry leaders?

- What support needs improvement?

- What steps can your church take to improve or enhance its support of your youth ministry?

Go for It!

Congregational commitment to and support for youth ministry is essential. Sure, youth ministry and how congregations provide support can be complex and challenging. Sometimes situations don't work out exactly as planned. Sometimes there is no easy solution to a problem. But that's typically the case in real life! You will have triumphs and challenges. Yet always consider the supports you have, build on them, and go for it!

As means of encouraging your further reflection on the status of your congregation's hope-building role, convene a congregational team to look at chart 9.1, "Youth Ministry—Triumphant or in Trouble?" on pages 206–207. The chart is intended to help you address the questions: In what ways is my congregation triumphant in its hope-building role? In what ways would I say my congregation is in trouble in its hope-building role? As a team, look carefully at each focal point on the chart. In the open boxes, decide on and check which ones apply to your church. Then answer the following questions:

• What did you check and why?

• What changes and improvements are needed?

• What actions need to be taken to improve or enhance the youth ministry?

In your review of the chart, you have likely noted that Youth ministry #1 seems to be in trouble. It suffers from minimal pastoral and parental support, and has a relatively small budget in contrast with the church size and number of participating youth. Although they have a paid youth ministry leader and some community support, their programs and youth involvement are sporadic and their future growth unspecified. Moreover, the youth minister does not appear to be cognizant of her or his youth base and infrequently assesses their needs. And without an annual program evaluation, it will be difficult to identify and subsequently respond to their problems. Although youth ministry #1 has some potentially impressive features (150 youth being just one of them), it has yet to take advantage of its potential in order to create and cultivate programs of promise.

Although youth ministry #2 can be considered a ministry of tri
umph, it also has some challenges to overcome. It benefits from
a supportive pastor, church, and parents as well as funding and
relatively committed youth. This is a solid program with a clear
mission statement, adequate youth-staff ratio, an evaluation plan
to assess outcomes, and documentation of projections, resources,
and efforts to make the ministry come alive for youth.

The above exercise helps us understand several realities:

• Despite some problems, your youth ministry can be triumphant.

• Most problems have solutions.

• Involvement by multiple people from the church and community may be necessary to solve some problems.

• Quality youth programs are not automatically a product of
church size, funds, or paid leadership.

• Even well-meaning churches can lapse in their ability to organize the types of programs needed to work with youth.

• Program evaluations are crucial for creating, maintaining, and
growing programs of promise.

Whether and how a youth ministry leader and the congregation respond to the above types of issues can be the difference between the ministry being a success or struggling. Proactive youth
ministry leaders and their congregations who have a big-picture
view of ministry combined with specific plans about how to ac-
complish it—and a clear evaluation method—are more likely
to develop a program that is beneficial for youth, parents, the
church, and the community.

Assure Out of the Box Teamwork Between
Youth Ministry and Congregational Leaders

Organizational studies can be used to aid congregations in helping
youth ministers cultivate hope-centered ministries. The studies can
also inform us about the types of actions and activities that make
youth ministry come alive for black youth! Studies suggest that

Chart 9.1. Youth Ministry—Triumphant or in Trouble?

Scenario	YM #1	Solution/ Strategy	YM #2	Solution/ Strategy
Vision Statement	Thought about it, but none at this time		"To respond holistically to the needs of youth as we show unconditional love"	
Pastoral Support and Involvement	Minimal and inconsistent		Strong and consistent	
Youth Involvement	150 youth (demographics unknown): low but steady participation (usually when food is provided)		85 youth (50 girls, 35 boys; average age is 12 years): high, falls off during summer, bounces back when school starts (even without food)	
Parental Support	Low		High	
Community Resources	Some support from local YWCA		Gets food donations from several local grocery stores	
Church Support	Somewhat, but largely lip service		High with both human and economic resources	
Church Demographics	2,000 active members		750 active members	
Youth Ministry Leader	Paid youth minister but really wishes to pastor		Volunteer youth minister, dedicated but sometimes drained	

teams are needed to effect successful organizational functioning. The most effective teams tend to include people with diverse backgrounds who also have diverse skills and experiences. This says something about a team of congregational leaders who are needed for successful youth ministry functioning. The team needs synergy that involves three steps: *mapping*, *bridging*, and *integrating*.[7] Each of these steps requires the team's imagination in order for youth ministry to move forward in transformative ways. The team must be comfortable thinking outside the box!

Chart 9.1. Youth Ministry—Triumphant or in Trouble? (continued)

Scenario	YM #1	Solution/ Strategy	YM #2	Solution/ Strategy
Staff Size	1 paid support staff and 5 volunteers (includes 2 parent volunteers)		1 paid support staff and 20 volunteers (includes 15 parent volunteers)	
Types of Programs	Quarterly Bible studies, monthly sleepovers, annual rap sessions to assess youth needs		Weekly Bible studies, weekly rap sessions to assess needs, monthly sleepovers, monthly "Day with the Pastor," monthly African/Black History Awareness events	
Budget	About $500 biannually, can request other funds if available		$2,000 annually (1 percent of the overall church budget)	
Plans for Ministry Growth	To be arranged, difficult to provide current programs		Goals: 4 percent growth each year: new canvass in nearby housing complex; quarterly workshops on conflict management and leadership skills	
Annual Program Evaluation	Talked about it, but has not materialized		Yes, has helped strengthen ministry, although all problems have not been rectified	

Mapping

Holistic, comprehensive programs of promise require a congregational team that includes youth ministry leaders, clergy, parents, youth, and community members. This can be a tall task because each group is different and brings different profiles, skill sets, experiences, and expectations to the encounter. Moreover, each person within each group is also diverse. But because persons are bound together by God's love and sincere desire to help black youth, characteristics that might confound secular organizations can represent opportunities and efforts to work together to cultivate excellent youth ministry. In such situations, thinking outside the box means understanding the diverse people who comprise the youth ministry team and what that their differences might mean for creating programs of promise. This is called *mapping*.

Bridging

Furthermore, an effective youth ministry team must engage in *bridging*. This means linking or connecting with one another in ways that assure a healthy relational aptitude and operational aptitude. It requires intentional and ongoing communication with all those persons who might impact youth programs and activities. In this regard, parents must not be left out. Revisit Chapter 8 on communication with parents. It also means that team members must understand and agree on the purpose of youth ministry and must understand each other if they expect to develop a process from which programs of promise can emerge and continue.

Integrating

Lastly, team members bring their different viewpoints, expectations, and plans together and work through intra-group challenges until the most appropriate types of youth ministry programs are created for their specific church and community. This *integrating* process begins by understanding and respecting that other people are different and bring different skills, strengths, and even baggage to youth ministry work. But the process of working with and through group challenges will ultimately result in youth programs that meet the diverse profiles, needs, and expectations of black youth.

Hope-centered youth ministry also requires youth leaders and their allies in and beyond the congregation to acknowledge and respond to issues of *centering*. What is this concept, and how does it relate to youth programs of promise? Even the sincerest, most dedicated youth ministry team members can get sidetracked by *self*—personal objectives for youth that can overshadow God's plan for them—or by church politics or clergy biases that impact consistent support for youth ministry. These unchecked tendencies can become the difference between a youth ministry that is triumphant and one that is constantly wracked by trials and tribulations.

Instead of centering on themselves, effective youth ministry leaders and team members must decenter or refocus attention back to the needs, concerns, and expectations of youth!

The two-step process of decentering and recentering will help insure that adults involved in youth ministry intentionally and constantly remind themselves that what they are doing is ultimately all about youth! The decentering step is about moving from a focus on self. In the heat of a problem or disagreements that arise, "getting the self out of the way" releases leaders and team members to recenter on what matters—the youth and ministry with them. When youth ministry leaders and other people involved in developing youth programs/activities are able to separate "the people from the problem" and consider things from the perspective of others (especially youth), programs of promise are sure to emerge.

✓CHECK IT OUT

Invite a team that includes the youth ministry leader, congregational leaders, some parent(s) and a youth to read and engage together the activities outlined in the chapter. Then, as a team, based on your reading and engagement of this chapter, enter into conversation on the question: What now is your plan for enlivening the hope-building power of your team and congregation? Take some time as a youth ministry team to explore your plan. End by affirming one another's part in making possible hope-centered ministry. Share words of encouragement with one another. End with a prayer for your journey forward on behalf of hope-centered youth ministry.

NOTES

1. Andrew Billingsley, *Climbing Jacob's Ladder: The Enduring Legacy of African-American Families* (New York: Touchstone, 1994).

2. C. Eric Lincoln and Lawrence H. Mamiya, *The Black Church in the African American Experience* (Durham, NC: Duke Univ. Press, 1990), 396.

3. Christian Smith, Melinda Lundquist Denton, Robert Faris, and Mark Regnerus, "Mapping American Adolescent Religious Participation," *Journal for the Scientific Study of Religion* 41, no. 4 (2002): 597–612.

4. Ronnie Prevost, "Creating the Undiscovered Country: Religious Education as an Agent of Forging the Third Millennium," 226–42, in James Michael

Lee, ed., *Forging a Better Religious Education in the Third Millennium* (Birmingham, AL: Religious Education Press, 2000), 241–42. Prevost points to the difficulties churches often have in communicating foundational beliefs in a contemporary fashion so that these beliefs are understood by new generations and speak to the issues of the present.

5. Helpful resources on intergenerational worship and ministry include Holly Catterton and Christine Lawton Ross, *Intergenerational Christian Formation: Bringing the Whole Church Together in Ministry, Community and Worship* (Downers Grove, IL: InterVarsity, 2012); Howard A. Vanderwell, *The Church of All Ages: Generations Worshiping Together* (Herndon, VA: Alban Institute, 2007); and Merton P. Strommen and Richard A. Hardel, *Passing On the Faith: A Radical New Model for Youth and Family Ministry* (Winona, MN: Saint Mary's Press, 2000).

6. Information on the report appears in: Barna Update, "Most Twentyseomthings Put Christianity on the Shelf Following Spiritually Active Teen Years," September 11, 2006, www.barna.org/teens-next-gen-articles/147-most-twentysthings-put-christianity-on-the-shelf/, accessed April 4, 2012.

7. Refer to Martha Maznevski and Joseph DiStefano, "Global Leaders Are Team Players," *Human Resource Management* 39, no. 2–3 (Summer–Fall 2000): 195–208.

EPILOGUE
Claiming Hope, Moving Forward

Let us hold fast to the confession of our hope without
wavering, for he who has promised is faithful.
—Hebrews 10:23

Daring to dream is the stuff that youth ministry is made of. In the prologue, we said that dreaming allows us to reach beyond what is going on right now in our youth ministry. Dreaming releases our imagination that enables us to see in the future the most amazing ministry that flows from our minds and hearts. Throughout each chapter, we have invited leaders and others involved in youth ministry to envision youth ministry possibilities and make decisions that take ministry beyond the possibilities to actual "wow" programs, practices, events, connections, attitudes, involvement, and commitments. In the introduction, we invited all who support youth ministry to "turn on the music and hit the floor" and to "enjoy dancing to your heart's content" in celebration of the promise, through inevitable challenges, but in sync with what God has in store.

Now it's time to claim the hope in God's promises and dance with the surety of that hope. How may we understand this claim and dance with surety? Let's consider seven movements of the dance of claiming hope for youth ministry leadership and youth ministry:

1. Reach out to receive and welcome youth
2. Attest to the certainty of what we receive
3. Accept the gift of service
4. Become responsible agents of hope
5. Celebrate the blessings that come from youth ministry
6. Claim the Source of the gift
7. Commit to a "village" dance that keeps hope alive

Reach Out to Receive and Welcome Youth

Young people are the reason for ministry that youth leaders and congregations undertake on their behalf. Claiming hope means demanding of ourselves actions that make youth a priority. When we claim hope, we assure holistic and relevant offerings for youth, guarantee necessary ministry supports, and ensure their formation of spiritual values and resilience needed for positive identity as Christians and black persons. Reaching out to black youth is a necessary claiming step that centers on welcoming them, knowing who they are, hearing them, and responding to the distinctive stories they live every day. Hope for their forward journey in life lies in what we do that helps them link their stories to God's story contained in Scripture and discover their life's purpose.

Attest to the Certainty of What We Receive

Claiming hope for our youth and for our ministry with them is not a casual happening. Leaders become certain of what is entailed in it because of a call to lead. We may have experienced God's voice calling us, felt a nudge to give back, or sensed a call to go beyond what we were already doing, or perhaps we were simply pressed into youth ministry service. Whatever the call, leaders are compelled to answer it because it is real. We cannot deny our call! We attest to the certainty of our call and what it means for receiving, welcoming, and serving today's youth.

Accept the Gift of Service

The act of claiming something entails accepting whatever is claimed as one's own. The one who claims recognizes that what is claimed is something important and special. When leaders and those who have a stake in youth ministry claim hope for our youth and ministry with them, we agree that this hope must be unwavering; and we hold fast to it because we know that what we do is in the hands of a faithful God (Hebrews 10:23). We hang in there through refreshing times of accomplishment and daunting times of challenge. We stay centered on the God who called us to it. There is no confusion about what we're supposed to do. We are conscious of the road ahead. We have a vision, and the call keeps us open to the ministry's unfolding story with readiness to see how the vision unfolds. We have courage in the line of fire. Of course, we know that today's youth ministry is not easy; and it is likely that it never was entirely trouble-free. Support may wane. Finances may be low or nonexistent. Success in developing relevant programs and activities may be elusive. Growing our group of youth and reaching unchurched youth may happen slowly or may not seem to happen at all. Arrival at our wits' end and the cliff that overlooks burnout happens.

Remembering and sometimes reaccepting our call, along with saying yes to the gift of our youth and ministry with them is the way forward. This acceptance gives us the nerve to continue—the holy boldness needed to move on. In that movement forward, we create times with God, engage in spiritual disciplines, and find times for renewal and recreation. We commit ourselves to go the length with youth and in ministry with them, for the sake of the gospel of Jesus Christ that we want them to know and live.

Become Responsible Agents of Hope

The act of claiming suggests that the one who does the claiming becomes responsible for what is claimed. In ministry with youth, leaders and all those who are connected with it become responsible for making the hope we claim come alive in everything we do. Leaders and congregations need relational know-how and

operational know-how to enliven hope. We must have the willingness to connect with youth, care for them, collaborate with them,
and celebrate their presence with us. We must show responsibility
by providing a welcoming environment that youth experience as
Sawubona (I see you) and to which they willingly respond with
Sikhona (I am here). Making all of this happen requires leaders
and congregations to know themselves and be honest about the
capabilities as well as the limitations they have.

Responsibility-taking happens further in the choices of programs and activities that leaders and congregations make to assure ministry relevance, excellence, and hope. Ministry program
choices rely on leaders' recognition that the world we live in today
is vastly different from the one of years ago! We live in a high-tech
world with high-tech communications with which our youth are
comfortable. If youth ministry leaders and our congregations are to
be relationship-tending agents of hope, we must relate with youth
using high-tech means, while at the same time assuring up-close,
person-to-person contact that today's youth need and crave. When
leaders and congregations take responsibility for youth ministry
programs, we also choose what will address the holistic needs of
our youth. This means choosing programs and materials that promote as much as possible youths' spiritual development, cultural
awareness and affirmation, social learning, environmental and political awareness, cognitive development and educational preparedness, emotional well-being, and physical development.

Taking responsibility extends to leaders' intentional preparation
in order to make good on our hope of moving forward and making
a hope-filled impact on the lives of youth. Leaders find both formal
and informal means of preparing and remaining tooled for excellent, hope-centered ministry leadership.

Celebrate the Blessings That Come from Youth Ministry

When something is claimed, however great or small and whether
under difficult circumstances, the one who claims it is glad and considers what is received as a blessing. In fact, the claiming act itself

can evoke a sense of awe, honor, surprise, and gratitude. It becomes a spiritual matter when the one who claims something knows that what is received could not have happened except by the grace of God. Youth ministry leaders often say that it is an honor to be called to ministry with youth. It is as though the hope that leaders claim for youth and ministry with them is returned a thousandfold. The blessings received from this ministry far exceed what we give. Leaders tie this experience to the passage in Luke that says, "Give, and it will be given to you. A good measure, pressed down, shaken together and running over, will be poured into your lap. For with the measure you use, it will be measured to you" (Luke 6:38 NIV).

The blessing resulting from hope claimed and hope made real in youth ministry is cause for celebration because of the blessing youth are to us and the value, giftedness, and promise that their being conveys. The cause for celebration is the opportunity given to leaders and congregations to be in ministry with and on their behalf. We celebrate our youth because of the life and energy they bring and our recognition that they are in our present and are our future.

Our celebration extends to appreciating our youth as a gift—God's gift—and our delight in their presence, honor in their accomplishments, and hope for their future. They need the affirmation that is part of our celebration. They need the care that must be a continuing outgrowth of celebration. And they deserve the radical healing that eludes far too many but that our leaders' and churches' celebration of hope must help to make possible.

Claim the Source of the Gift

God is the Source of the gift of ministry with youth, the youth we serve in it, and all that is undertaken as part of it. Congregations and leaders are called into this ministry by God. Claiming God as the Source of every hope-centered aspect of youth ministry means that we declare—profess—God as the One who calls us to it. At the center of this declaration is our knowing that our vision, energies, and hope emerging from the call come from God. This Source anchors us in who and Whose we are and, through Jesus Christ, is our sure foundation and anchor of our hope (Hebrews 6:19). We are reminded by one of the leaders in the Vision Quest study that claiming God as the Source of the gift of ministry that is given to us "releases inspiration from God, direction from Jesus, and energy from the Holy Spirit." With their words, other leaders recount to us the importance of God along our ministry journey:

- "We wouldn't get very far in this ministry without loving trust and hope in God's being with us every step of the way."

- "Our knowing and feeling the Spirit of the ever-present One allows us to holler, 'Help me Holy Ghost' in those moments that inevitably come when we're at our wits end."

- "God gives us the motivation that fuels our leadership, keeps us going, and makes us say, 'I have to do it!' Ministry readiness comes from God's gift of 'holy boldness' and sometimes dangerous courage needed to get the job done!"

In our claiming God as gift-giving Source, we profess God as our constant spiritual resource. We seek ongoing connection—an up-close relationship—with this Source! Recall from the introduction that our daily walk in youth ministry leadership becomes wholly hope-centered only to the extent that we are intentional in our prayer life, times of meditation, study of Scripture, and engagement in other spiritual disciplines like journaling, fasting, and tending to our wellness.

Commit to a Village Dance That Keeps Hope Alive

Claiming hope for our youth and ministry with them is meant to result in youth who are unapologetically Christian and unashamedly black. This is the undertaking of an entire village. This mission is not the sole action of the youth ministry leader. Claiming hope becomes translated into the actions of parents and entire congregations, who commit to serve youth within and beyond the church walls. There is no "us" and "them" but, rather, a community that is conscious of the interdependent parts of youth ministry programs and activities, and the interdependence of the people and youth who are already or must become participants. The African proverb is true: "It takes a village to raise a child." But it is also true that if we believe we are one body with many members, as the apostle Paul describes it in 1 Corinthians 12, then we belong together, are indispensable to one another, and must move together in a holy dance through which hope comes and is kept alive in every move by the power of the Holy Spirit. May it be so!